WHEN THE HEAVENS ARE

BRASS

PRACTICAL KEYS TO EXPERIENCING GENUINE REVIVAL

JOHN KILPATRICK

DESTINY IMAGE® PUBLISHERS, INC.

P.O. Box 310, Shippensburg, PA 17257-0310

Promoting Inspired Lives.

Previously published as *When the Heavens Are Brass* by Destiny Image
Previous ISBN: 1-56043-190-3

This book and all other Destiny Image and Destiny Image Fiction books are available at Christian bookstores and distributors worldwide.

For more information on foreign distributors, call 717-532-3040.

Reach us on the Internet: www.destinyimage.com.

ISBN 13 TP: 978-0-7684-6245-6
ISBN 13 eBook: 978-0-7684-6246-3
ISBN 13 HC: 978-0-7684-6248-7
ISBN 13 LP: 978-0-7684-6247-0

For Worldwide Distribution, Printed in the U.S.A.
1 2 3 4 5 6 7 8 / 26 25 24 23 22

ACKNOWLEDGMENTS

As a revival pastor, I appreciated the diligence of faithful workers under what most people would consider impossible circumstances. Revival only comes where unity in the Spirit is found. Most people familiar with the Brownsville Revival think of my close friends of many years, Evangelist Steve Hill and anointed psalmist Lindell Cooley, or me. Our faces were the ones most often seen on the platform during the revival services, in magazine articles, and on videotapes. However, it took hundreds of people's cooperation and dedicated efforts to take care of the hard labor of practical ministry necessary for the meetings. The diligent labor of many unseen and often unthanked servants of God opened the door for the Holy Spirit to move freely among people in each service.

Each time I saw Rose Compton in the congregation, I wondered what I would do without such an able administrative assistant. Who else could have worked so well and so smoothly with more than 350 trained workers who so faithfully served night after night? Every time I glanced to my left, I saw Bill Bush, the head usher, with his wife, Jeanie. Bill volunteered countless hours coordinating 75 of the most outstanding ushers I have ever known. Night after night, Steve Whitehead and his loyal crew of cameramen and technicians amazed me; thanks to them, every moment of the revival was captured on videotape and audiotape. Our security team and volunteer plainclothes police officers helped meet the safety concerns of the thousands who attended the nightly services.

In the next section of pews, I saw my beloved wife, Brenda. God started the revival fire in my wife before the fire started in me; it made me jealous to go after God to get what she had. Sitting near my precious Brenda was Lila Terhune, head of our intercessors. The diligent R.L. Berry was our church treasurer, trusted friend, and was always faithful. Cheryl Grayson, in the balcony, was adept in managing our pastors' conferences. When I looked across the balcony, I would see Teresa Castleman. Her deliverance teams spent hour upon hour in personal ministry, praying for people to be set free from the bondage of past sins.

Each time I saw Elmer Melton and the members of our fine Board of Directors, or any of our more than 20 deacons, I was strengthened and encouraged. I was grateful to God for people like the lovable Randy Worrell, who visited the sick and ministered to the bedridden, for our faithful interpreters for the deaf, for Vann Lane, our dedicated and dynamic children's pastor. Joining me on the platform, along with Steve Hill and Lindell Cooley, were our worship team, our ever-faithful choir, and orchestra. Then there was our energetic youth pastor, Richard Crisco; my trusted associate minister, Carey Robertson; my Jewish teacher and friend, Dick Reuben; and the president of our Bible school, Dr. Michael Brown. When revival came to Brownsville, God did a work in all our lives. As it ended, we had a greater love and hunger for Him than ever before.

CONTENTS

FOREWORD

What a high honor it was to work with Evangelist Steve Hill for the duration of the Brownsville Revival. He was a soldier of the Cross, a passionate and powerful preacher, and a wonderful ministry companion. We were in over 2,000 services together. When we came together, it truly was God-ordained because it just worked. I'm honored to present to you the original foreword Steve wrote for this book's first publication in 1997.

—JOHN A. KILPATRICK

John Kilpatrick has been in the pastoral ministry for more than 25 years. I have had the privilege of knowing him personally for 13 of those years. He is not only a dear friend but also a biblical pastor in the fullest sense of the word.

It is virtually impossible to plow along in the field of ministry for any period of time without experiencing major disappointment and incredible victories—and everything in between. John Kilpatrick's road to revival has been full of bends, turns, hills, stop signs, and, of course, lots of traffic.

He has fought "bull" demons from hell and experienced firsthand the warfare of the enemy. Victory has come—and continues to come—with a price. William Bramwell once said, "Never look for peace while you proclaim war." John Kilpatrick has proclaimed war. He has planted his feet firmly in the trenches, vigilantly protecting his flock and fighting to the end for the salvation of souls.

This book, *When the Heavens Are Brass,* is timely. America and the world are on the verge of a widespread awakening. We need to be alerted to the fact that a price must be paid in order to break through the enemy's lines and plunder his camp. I encourage the reader to heed the words of the late Leonard Ravenhill: "Don't just go through this book, but let this book go through you."

May the Lord open the eyes of your spiritual mind and enable you to grasp the truths in this much-needed book.

Stephen Hill, Evangelist
Together in the Harvest Ministries

INTRODUCTION

Corporate businessmen in expensive suits knelt and wept uncontrollably as they repented of secret sins. Drug addicts and prostitutes fell to the floor on their faces to lie prostrate before God as they confessed Jesus as Lord for the first time in their lives. Reserved, elderly women and weary young mothers danced unashamedly before the Lord with joy. They were forgiven! Young children saw incredible visions of Jesus; their faces were a picture of divine delight framed by slender arms raised heavenward.

I saw these scenes replayed service after service and week after week during the Brownsville Revival. I knew that this was the fruit of a seven-year journey in prayer and two and a half years of fervent corporate intercession by the church family at Brownsville Assembly of God in Pensacola, Florida.

The souls who came to Christ, repenting and confessing their sin, the marriages restored, the many people freed from bondage that had long held them captive—these were the marks of revival and trophies of God's glory. I am not speaking of a revival that lasted one weekend, one week, one month, or even one year. The "Brownsville Revival" continued unbroken for five years—except for brief holiday breaks—from Father's Day 1995 to 2000! How? Only God knows. Why? First, because it was God's good pleasure, and second, perhaps the soil of our hearts was prepared in prayer long before revival came.

On that ordinary Sunday morning in June 1995, I was scheduled to minister but was weary. I was still trying to adjust to the recent loss of my mother, and my many years of desire for revival seemed to be so distant that morning. So I asked my friend, Evangelist Steve Hill, to fill the pulpit in my place. Although he was scheduled to speak in the evening service, Steve agreed to preach the Father's Day message that morning. We didn't know it then, but God was at work in every detail of that meeting.

The worship was ordinary (our worship leader, Lindell Cooley, was still ministering on a mission trip to Ukraine), and Steve Hill's message didn't seem to ignite any sparks—until the noon hour struck. When he gave an altar call, *suddenly,* God visited our congregation in a way we had never experienced. A thousand people came forward for prayer after his message. That was almost half of our congregation! Little did we know that our lives were about to change in a way we could never have imagined.

We knew better than to hinder such a move of God, so services continued day after day. We adjusted with incredible speed. During the first month, hundreds of people walked the aisles to repent. By the sixth month, thousands had responded to nightly altar calls. By the time we reached the twelfth month, 30,000 people had come to the altar to repent of their sins.

Hundreds of thousands of souls came to the altars and had a salvation experience—so many that we stopped counting. The crowds attending were so overwhelming that we couldn't keep up with the numbers. A safe, conservative estimate is that 4.5 million people attended. Tens of thousands were baptized in the Holy Spirt, and thousands were called into the ministry. Visitors came from every corner of the earth to drink of God's revival river. The local newspaper was quick to write very favorable articles about "The Brownsville Outpouring," and national Christian magazines were soon to follow suit.

Almost every month, chartered airliners filled with people from England, Canada, Norway, Germany, Japan, Korea, Scotland, New Zealand, Australia, Finland, and countless other countries landed at the Pensacola Airport. Many of these people came because churches in their nation pooled their resources to send representatives to Brownsville, hoping they would bring the fire of revival back to their homeland. Our local law enforcement officials had to make some interesting adjustments to accommodate the revival. They first noticed something different when reports of traffic jams and erratic drivers filtered into police stations. When going home from revival services, drivers who shook or appeared drunk while driving were commonplace. The officers who stopped these vehicles would many times just wave the people on when they heard, "We've been to Brownsville" or, "It's the Lord."

Before and After

Before the revival, our church had grown to a congregation of nearly two thousand. We had a healthy respect for Bible preaching and godly living. All the usual ministries were functioning in our fellowship, along with a television outreach program. This sounds wonderful, but I wasn't satisfied. I had a deep longing in my soul for more of God's presence and power. Many were far from God, and my pastor's heart burned for the numerous people in my congregation who were still in bondage.

The longing for more led me to a deeper prayer journey seven years before the revival descended in June 1995. During those early struggles, God began to instruct me through His Word about the nature of prayer and why "the heavens were brass." Of course, many prayers were answered during that time; but sometimes, the heavens seemed to be made of impenetrable brass. In the depths of my being, there burned a hunger for God, for more of His holy presence that only a feast of fire could satisfy.

Once revival came, thousands of visiting pastors, evangelists, and church leaders confessed to me that they had the same desperate hunger for God and had experienced the same frustration regarding "heavens of brass." I am convinced that the answers I received and put into practice during that seven-year prayer journey were part of God's plan to lay a foundation for revival. Revival is imminent when consistent prayer and intercession have prevailed. Revival will not come until God's people yield themselves to be changed and prepared through the persistence of fervent prayer.

Perhaps the most irrefutable proofs of revival were the written testimonies of people whose lives were transformed by God's power. These stories came in through email and letters, bringing incredible miracles to light.

A mother reported that her oldest son and his wife were born again. A father wrote about the conversion of his ten-year-old son. A young woman happily related how she was born again, baptized with water, filled with the Holy Spirit, and healed of a chronic infection within one month of attending the revival meetings. A respected businessman told of the brokenness that haunted him because of his early years of suffering sexual abuse. He rejoiced in the delivering power of Jesus Christ that healed him and set him free!

From the baptismal pool, two lesbians confessed Christ as their Lord and Savior, renounced their sin, and asked the son they had raised together for forgiveness. The young man said to his mother, "Oh, Mom. My prayers have been answered." These two gloriously saved and delivered women immediately moved to separate living quarters. Both new believers worked for a large corporation in the Pensacola area and were well known. They proclaimed the Gospel of their risen Lord and His power to deliver. Their testimonies had a profound effect on those who knew them.

Many reports of healing also accompanied the revival. A young man with a pinhole in a heart valve told of his total healing. An older woman who struggled with partial hearing in her right ear for a quarter of a century was instantly healed while standing at the altar area. A woman with pyelonephritis and kidney damage since childhood fell under the power of God. As she lay on the carpet, she felt a popping sensation in her side. When she finally stood up, she was free from pain and inflammation for the first time in years! A nurse had suffered severe lung damage for two long years. She had spent $10,000 just for her prescription drugs, not counting the other mounting medical bills. After attending the revival meetings, the nurse returned home to her husband and children in complete health. She no longer had to depend on expensive drugs to ease her pain and help her breathe.

A mother wrote to confess that she had considered suicide, but "for some reason" she and her husband attended the revival. They came to the altar together to repent of their sins and commit their lives to Jesus. "Never in my life have I known such joy," she wrote. "I keep praising the Lord and thanking Him."

Revival Spreads

So many pastors and ministers came to the revival that we decided to hold semi-annual pastors' conferences. Nearly 680 ministers attended the first conference held in November 1995, only five months after the revival began. The second pastors' conference, in April of 1996, ministered to nearly 1,400 registrants. In November of that year, the third conference was flooded by 2,029 hungry, on-fire-for-God pastors from almost every denomination. Each of these conferences helped us to see our dream come to pass—I believe it was God's dream too. As these pastors took the fire of revival home to their congregations and communities, it caused the revival to explode beyond geography, religious denomination, and nationality.

When the Heavens Are Brass

Despite the many who were blessed by God's revival fire, not everyone stepped into His mighty river of refreshing. Some still have a growing thirst for God's presence that has not yet been quenched. Others rejected the move of God's Spirit, which has happened many times before during great awakenings and historical revivals. Still others lost hope that the revival Spirit would touch them. Although the fire of revival spread to certain churches and cities, there were still far more who continued to struggle under a heaven of brass without a single flicker of hope for the fire of revival. I can't walk away from these brothers and sisters who are still staggering under the weight of the same burden I once carried. The heartbreaking telephone calls received from desperate pastors of declining churches, who have little faith for a breakthrough, are etched in my memory.

Why was it that the fires of revival came to some but did not spread to others? Perhaps you've also asked this question. You may be reading this book because you want to experience a personal Pentecost or you long to bring genuine revival to your family, ministry, or church. I want to share what I learned during the seven years before the revival came to Brownsville. Before God visited us in 1995, I grew weary of the hype that often floods our churches. I was tired of attending fabricated revivals woven together by carefully orchestrated services. These services were more dependent on the ability to impress than on the anointing of God that is birthed only in prayer and travail.

It was during those years of spiritual hunger and searching that God opened my eyes to see why the heavens had become brass and revival seemed so distant. He used these years of prayer, fasting, and longing for true revival to teach me how to pray more effectively. The congregation joined me in this pilgrimage of fervent intercession. Today, I can tell you with great joy that our journey in prayer had an exciting destination! The truths I learned about prayer and brass heavens laid the foundation for revival and a fresh understanding of God's *kabod,* the Hebrew term for His glory or "weightiness." These things have been tried and tested in the laboratory of life. They are illuminated and animated by the fruits, experiences, and insights we received when God so gloriously visited us on Father's Day 1995.

God is no respecter of persons. In the mid-1990s, Dr. David Yonggi Cho gave a prophecy emphatically stating that revival would begin at the seaside city of Pensacola, Florida and burn like a matchhead there first. It would travel westward to the River of the Holy Spirit (Mississippi River) and go back eastward along the Gulf Coast again. It would then sweep up the East Coast, across the Midwest to the West Coast, and all of America would be ablaze with the glory of God before the coming of Christ. I am longing for this prophecy to be fulfilled during our lifetime. Who knows, this may result in another spiritual great awakening in America.

Revival comes only from God. It is not the product of a program, system, or formula. Prayer and fasting can prepare the soil, but the Lord of the harvest alone decides how and when He will come. Still, we know He loves to meet with those who seek Him. This book describes how we sought Him and the lessons we learned about prayer. May God richly bless you with the fullness of His Holy Spirit as you pursue Him with all your heart, soul, mind, and strength. Be encouraged! I believe revival is coming soon!

CHAPTER 1

DEVILISH DOMINION UNDER A HEAVEN OF BRASS

I remember reading about a church where the power of God flowed in a wonderful stream of glory. The people enjoyed rich worship full of exuberance and joy. When they said, "Praise the Lord!" they meant it with all their hearts. Their words didn't resonate a bit like the "sounding brass and tinkling cymbals"[1] we hear so much in Christian circles today.

They sang songs with meaning, and the Spirit of God moved so powerfully during the song services that people often got up on their own without an altar call and walked to the altar to pray. When the old silver-haired pastor finally stood to preach, no one noticed that his voice was almost gone from years of heartfelt, Spirit-inspired preaching. He preached with depth and a rich sense of the grace of God, strengthened by the certainty that intercessors and prayer warriors were praying for him and those in need.

These praying men and women knew how to touch God. They spent much of the week secreted away in prayer closets or bedrooms, praying and interceding, "O God, when our pastor stands to minister, let the anointing be on him! Let Your power be there to draw people to You." They weren't interested in being elevated above others or being seen or heard by appreciative audiences. Their greatest joy, and source of fulfillment, came when they got alone with God and prayed fervently until God saved souls.

When the pastor decided to retire, the church's history was forever changed. Little did the people understand that not only was the ministry of their beloved pastor ending, but the vitality of their church was also coming to an end. Over the years, they had known the depths of the rich anointing and outpouring of the Holy Ghost. Solid Bible preaching and godly leadership had embedded a strong foundation in *most* of the congregation, drawing them ever closer to their Lord and His will.

Unfortunately, this was not true for *all* members of the congregation. The individuals on the pulpit committee felt that certain changes needed to be made. When they began searching for a new pastor, they all agreed to look for a very young man. They also decided that it was time to do away with some of the emotionalism in worship, especially the groaning and travailing of the intercessors. The committee had no difficulty finding a preacher who met their qualifications. Sadly, they never bothered to ask God what *His* qualifications might be.

Carnal Leadership Brings Heavens of Brass

The candidate chosen by the pulpit committee perfectly matched their list of qualifications. There was little of the irritating emotionalism they so wanted to avoid when he preached, and the congregation seemed amazingly docile. The committee found the peace quite refreshing; however, one irritation remained. At the end of the service, the former pastor's most elderly and faithful intercessor continued to leave her seat, kneel at the same two worn spots on the carpet where her fragile knees had knelt for so many decades, and plead for souls.

The new pastor was quite uncomfortable with the intercession of this elderly saint. Indeed, the altar call was the most challenging part of his duties when this godly woman began to intercede before God and publicly travail, "My God, send us revival! My God, give us souls this morning! Don't let souls leave here and go to hell!" So disturbed was the new pastor that he was strongly considering discarding this politically incorrect and somewhat primitive religious ritual from the order of service. He felt that there was something spooky about it all. The former pastor, on the other hand, had looked forward to this dear saint's prayer, knowing that it poured from the heart of God. It was the Spirit of God praying and travailing through this godly woman. Unfortunately, no Bible college had ever covered these subjects with the new pastor.

The young pastor endured this public spectacle for almost six months, but he took action one Sunday morning after finishing his sermon. As usual, the dear old sister was down on her knees travailing. So lost was she in intercession that she didn't even realize the pastor ended his sermon without giving an altar call. "Oh God, oh God," she cried, her little wrinkled face wet with tears.

The young pastor tapped the elderly intercessor on the shoulder and said, "Honey, there won't be any more need for that. We don't want that in this church because it hinders new-comers. They just don't understand it." The pastor didn't know it, but by his ignorant actions that day, he posted an ancient Hebrew name *Ichabod* over the church's front door. This means "the glory of the Lord has departed."[2]

Where Is the Touch of God?

Today, you can go into any average church and hear a minister preach with great oratorical ability. You can listen to the resonance of his trained voice and observe his posture. The average church has everything: the building, technology, volunteers, and staff. It is a well-oiled machine. There is a particular attentiveness to every detail of ministry that a church offers, but my question is, *where is the presence of God?*

America's churches compete with one another to draw the rich and famous and to fill their seats with the elite movers and shakers of their cities. Nearly every upscale neighborhood is dotted with new, user-friendly church buildings that are carefully designed to appeal to and draw the highest numbers of socially acceptable attendees. Still, the attendance of churches continues to drop, and the moral climate of our nation has virtually hit bottom. Christians are barely distinguishable from non-Christians, and the Church and her leaders are held in the highest contempt. In truth, our eyes are on ourselves, while God's eyes are on the many souls that hang in the balance. Something is terribly wrong. Unless somebody rediscovers how to touch God and is willing to pay the high price of revival, true revival will only be something we remember from bygone days.

> God never puts revival on sale. He never discounts it. It always costs the same for every generation.

Prayer is in disfavor across the land. Some say, "It just doesn't work." Others say, "It requires too much effort." Yet many sincere people are frustrated because their prayers are not answered. They even repeat a biblical phrase when they tell me, "When I pray, it almost seems like the heavens are brass. I just don't know what's wrong." After years of prayer and searching, I have discovered that "heavens of brass" perfectly describes the crisis of the Church in this hour! Breaking through heavens of brass is the key to revival.

Disobedience Causes a Heaven of Brass

The Church is losing the battle for men's souls. Many Christians will quickly admit that they spend most of their days living in virtual defeat, almost as if they live under a cloud all the time. The truth is—they do! We have overlooked the fact that the Bible describes echelons or hierarchies of powers, rulers, and evil principalities in the heavens, which impede the progress of the Church on the earth. Our disobedience increases this demonic power over us. To help us understand this more easily, let's look at some of the blessings and curses God declared to physical Israel (the nation) and spiritual Israel (the Church) in the Book of Deuteronomy.

The Blessing

> *And all these blessings shall come on thee, and overtake thee, if thou shall hearken unto the voice of the Lord thy God. Blessed shalt thou be in the city, and*

blessed shalt thou be in the field (Deuteronomy 28:2-3).

The Curse

But it shall come to pass, if thou wilt not hearken unto the voice of the Lord thy God...thy heaven that is over thy head shall be brass, and the earth that is under thee shall be iron (Deuteronomy 28:15, 23).

We have forgotten that hordes of demonic spirit-beings led by Satan are doing everything in their power to pull us down to their level of diabolical depravity. The apostle Paul made it clear that most of his battles were against *spiritual* foes.[3] Demonic powers were the real force motivating, guiding, and empowering the men and institutions that hindered the work of God in the first century. This is still true today, but we don't realize it because the Church, by and large, has abandoned the ways of the Spirit in favor of the traditions of men. It is no accident that we are continually defeated in many areas, including marriages, homes, churches, and nations.

Most Christian work is done in the physical (natural) realm because we think and act like we are dealing with mere mortal men. We exploit every new method we can dream up to turn our churches into a "home and garden" religion. We want everything to be nice and tidy. We don't want any discomfort or confrontation, so we carefully avoid the conviction of sin. We put on stage productions and call in the latest and most excellent speakers. We post media online and broadcast our services. However, we seldom think about dealing with the *strongman* who rules so many lives and communities! Unless these demonic forces are understood and dealt with, they will undoubtedly hinder the move of God's Spirit.

We are blind to the problem in the heavens because we are focused on the "seen" instead of the "unseen." We work through men to reach men instead of asking the Spirit of God to move on men's hearts to bring them to their knees.

What would happen if we abandoned our useless man-made methods to reach the lost? What would happen if we cried out in the name of Jesus, who alone has the power and authority to disarm principalities and rulers of darkness? This is an essential key for breaking through brass heavens! As we turn from the ways of man and cling to the power of God, we will see men's hearts changed, their bodies healed, and their lives mended.

Over the last decade, I learned that we do not please God when we do things our way. He is weary of hearing us blame Him for not blessing our mess. We have no right to complain when we stubbornly lean on our man-made methodologies rather than on the raw power of fervent prayer. If we want genuine revival, we must do things God's way. Period.

> God has fixed life so that
> it won't work without Him.

God warned us that if we fail to do things His way, *"thy* [your] *heaven that is over thy* [your] *head shall be brass."*[4] What "heaven" is God talking about, and how can it be brass?

Let's look closely at this verse. God was talking about *your* heaven that is over *your* head. Heaven can be open to you without being open to the one standing beside you. Jesus expressed this principle in Matthew 24:40:

> *Then shall two be in the field; the one shall be taken, and the other left.*

Heaven was open over one person in the field but closed over the other.

Many years ago, there was a popular comic strip named "Pogo." One of the characters in the strip always had a black cloud hovering above him. No matter where he went or what he did, he had his personal black cloud just over his head. This may be one of the most accurate portrayals of a brass heaven we will ever see. If we believe the lies of the devil, we put our futures, families, and churches into his hands and allow him to shut the heavens over our heads. Paul warned us not to give place to the devil.[5]

Sin Makes the Heavens Brass

Here in the southern United States, we say that sour milk has "clabbered" once curds appear since it has thickened and grown cloudy. Sin does the same to the heavens. Sin thickens the heavens so that they eventually become hardened to our prayers like brass is hardened and made resistant to fire and pressure. Sin separates us from the purity and openness of God's provision.

The Bible says:

> *In the beginning God created the heaven and the earth* (Genesis 1:1).

The heavens were clean. There was no spiritual pollution—no hierarchy or echelons of demons, powers, principalities, or dark rulers in the heavens—affecting the earth. God looked at the twinkling stars, planets, and vast expanse of the heavens He made and pronounced them good.

Later, Adam sinned and relinquished his God-given authority to the devil. That gave Satan a new title in his function as the leaseholder and chief governing authority of this fallen planet. Paul told the Ephesians:

> *In time past ye walked according to the course of this world, according to the prince of the power of the air, the spirit that now worketh in the children of disobedience* (Ephesians 2:2).

In the beginning, God communicated with His creation without hindrance. The sin of Adam brought separation and limited dialogue between God and man. Each generation wandered further from God until Noah recognized the voice of his Maker. During the great flood, a whole generation was shut out from the ark and from God. After this, Noah's descendants quickly forgot God's voice, so God began to search for a man He could talk to, and He found Abram. Through Abram's faith, God once again gained entrance into the affairs of men. Covenant was established, and even to this day, nearly 4,000 years later, God still passes the blessings of Abraham down to us.[6]

Our sin significantly impairs our ability to receive these blessings because it impedes our prayers and prevents us from hearing the voice of God's Spirit deep in our hearts. Sin gives

Satan the authority to come in and rule over us. The devil cannot do anything unless we give him the power. Persistent, willful sin provides the devil that power. Adam legally mortgaged this world system to the devil through sin. He bartered man's divine birthright for a taste of Satan's evil.

Satan immediately went to work like he was playing a cosmic game of "Monopoly." He quickly developed a sinister master plan, assessing where and how he would establish strongholds and what he would use to lure God's fallen creatures into his territory. His obvious objective was to accumulate as much as possible, as quickly as possible. No tactic was absent from his arsenal of weapons. Deception, lies, and dulled minds—these were but a few of the traps Satan used to entice men into his kingdom.

Some human institutions yielded quickly to his influence, allowing Satan to amass significant wealth and authority. Others have been slower to yield control into his hand and have resisted his demands more successfully. Still, even on the fringes of the devil's kingdom, his power and influence are consistently felt.

However, I believe redeemed saints will regain control of what the devil has taken by confessing their sins and obeying God's Word. Land that was once under the dominion of Satan will once again become holy ground. Although holy places have been disappearing for years, a revival of God's presence in the earth will bring them back.

Historically, the Church has squandered her strength. She has given in to distractions and infighting. She has been lured by this world's riches and dulled by impotent religion. She has given the devil every opportunity to consolidate his power over the nations.

Years before the Brownsville Revival, I felt Satan was trying to establish a strong principality over the Pensacola area. I sensed Satanism, witchcraft, greed, and sexual lusts settling over the area for an extended siege. Today, it is clear that Satan is still trying to firmly set up powerful principalities over cities and localities.

I encountered such evil dominion when my wife, Brenda, and I were en route to San Bernardino, California, from Phoenix, Arizona. Crossing the desert just before entering the San Bernardino area, I felt my spirit suddenly begin to shrivel and shrink as an awful heaviness tried to settle on me. Brenda felt the oppression too.

At a later date, we invited a friend from San Jose, California, to preach at the church we were pastoring. During a casual conversation, this man said, "You know, John, San Bernardino is one of the strongest centers of witchcraft in the nation—as a matter of fact, in the world!" He had my undivided attention because I remembered the oppression I felt that dark night in the desert outside of San Bernardino. He said, "There are more ritualistic sacrifices conducted in that desert area than in any other place in the nation." My spirit had picked up the presence and evil influence of a demonic strongman hovering over that city and region.

I have sensed the same kind of oppression in many key cities across America, especially New Orleans. Some of the most powerful men of God in our day, whom we love, have "met their Waterloo" under the powerful influence of the lustful strongman seated over that city. Is everyone in New Orleans dominated by evil spirits? *Absolutely not!* I have many personal friends who are strong Christians and ministers there. However, wherever an evil strongman is seated in authority, Christians and churches encounter greater resistance. It becomes more challenging to win the lost because of the extreme power wielded by the hellish influence overhead.

I have felt helpless at times as I have seen how the devil successfully entangles the Church. He leads her astray with grand distractions and diversions. He turns her attention from worshiping God to things that are not God's. Some have even made an idol of their one-time salvation experience, worshiping it in place of the God of their salvation. We act like once we receive our ticket to Heaven, we can do anything we want in any way we think is right. We have become content to casually worship a God that we hardly know. We have forgotten His Word and no longer seek Him in the cool of the evening. We go our own way and expect Him to meet us there, but He cannot and will not bless sin, selfishness, or rebellion! If there is sin in our lives, the heavens will remain brass over our heads, and Satan will increase the territory under his dominion. Only prayer, coupled with obedience, can stop his desperate bid for power.

When Jesus was born in Bethlehem, the heavens were brass. Prayer and obedience were His keys to break through the brass and hear His Father's voice. Through His sinless life and ministry, it was incumbent upon Christ to reveal to mankind how to open closed heavens. Sin and religious tradition ruled the day. All that was about to change because our Lord's obedience to His Father's will and His powerful intercession blasted a hole in the brass heavens.

> *Who in the days of his flesh, when he had offered up prayers and supplications with strong crying and tears unto him that was able to save him from death, and was heard in that he feared; though he were a Son, yet learned he obedience by the things which he suffered; and being made perfect, he became the author of eternal salvation unto all them that obey him* (Hebrews 5:7-9).

The Absence of Prayer Produces a Heaven of Brass

Today we are at a disadvantage because there are not as many faithful saints bombarding Heaven as in days gone by. This nation has become so self-centered and pleasure-minded that we have neglected to pray. We are so distracted caring for our own affairs that we are failing to seek the face of God. The heavens have hardened. Our prayers go unanswered, and the power of God is no longer evident in the earth.

In 1989, the Lord spoke to my heart and said, "Son, warn the Church to pray. Tell My people to start praying, for the heavens that were once clear and yielding are now becoming brass." That warning is more urgent today than it was then. Of all times, we must pray now! We must pray under the anointing and with great courage. We must recognize we are dealing with demonic entities such as principalities, rulers of darkness, and ranks of beings of which we have little knowledge. Their purpose is to hinder supernatural intervention with humanity. The Church needs fresh revelation on how to open the heavens.

Those who persevere in their pursuit of God will be victorious and known in hell, as were the first apostles. Peter, the fisherman, persevered through his failures and shortcomings. He persevered through the pain of guilt when he betrayed his Lord. He endured the Lord's loving correction after His resurrection. Later, he became Peter the apostle, who exercised absolute authority over demons in Jesus' name. When others who had not paid the price of submission and total dedication to Christ tried to exercise authority over demons as Peter had done, they discovered that they were not known in hell.

> *Then certain of the vagabond Jews, exorcists, took upon them to call over them which had evil spirits the name of the Lord Jesus, saying, We adjure you by Jesus whom Paul preacheth. And there were seven sons of one Sceva, a Jew, and chief of the priests, which did so. And the evil spirit answered and said, Jesus I know, and Paul I know; but who are ye? And the man in whom the evil spirit was leaped on them, and overcame them, and prevailed against them, so that they fled out of that house naked and wounded. And this was known to all the Jews and Greeks also dwelling at Ephesus; and fear fell on them all, and the name of the Lord Jesus was magnified* (Acts 19:13-17).

Remove the Obstacles to Revival

As we entered the 1990s, I realized how desperately I wanted more of God. I ached to see the lost saved, but I felt powerless and ineffective. I felt like our congregation was powerless too, even though we had been praying regularly. This sense of powerlessness changes only when we resolve to remove the obstacles to revival that make the heavens brass over our heads.

I used to pastor in a rural area where an elderly farmer in my church had a three-acre fishing pond on his property. One day the water supply that fed into the pond became clogged, and the water stopped flowing. Within a short time, all the teeming amphibious life in that pond died from suffocation, and the algae took over. After a while, that beautiful little fishing pond was reduced to a stinking cesspool. When the farmer unclogged the water source, the life-giving flow was restored, and life eventually returned to that pond.

Our lives are like that stagnant pond. We are denied the life-giving presence and power of God because we have allowed carnal leadership in our homes and our churches. Our disobedience, sin, and lack of prayer have clogged our fellowship with our Source. Remember, the devil only exercises authority when it is given to him. Only repentance and an unrelenting pursuit of God will break his power and rescue our cities and nations from his dominion.

I don't know how much of a stronghold the devil has on America, but God isn't finished with this nation. I sense a fracturing taking place. Breakthrough is beginning! God dearly loves the people of this nation and is sounding a wake-up call to our churches! He has already paid the price for our freedom. Now, He is asking us, "Will you pay the price to save your land?"

Bow Your Knee

The Word says:

> *Submit yourselves therefore to God. Resist the devil,*
> *and he will flee from you* (James 4:7).

Our problem is that we conveniently forget the first half of that verse! We like the "fleeing" part but avoid the "submitting" part like the plague. The truth is that no fleeing will occur until the submitting takes place. If the devil isn't fleeing from you, don't blame God. If you want the enemy to flee, you must yield. You must submit to God.

If we fail to bow our knees before God, the heavens over our heads will remain brass. This will be evident everywhere. There will be few conversions to Christ, and we will not see hungry people being baptized in the Holy Ghost. True revival will not come.

We cannot afford not to have true revival! I don't know about you, but I have seen so much painted fire (an imitation of true revival), and I have seen so much smoke from work born in man's head instead of God's heart that it disgusts me! We hear people talk about revival, but we often discover that their "rain clouds" have not rained a drop. Oh, there was some thunder and flashes of lightning, but true revival was nowhere to be found. Those clouds never gave rain! People were left out as dry as ever—there was no change; therefore, they are again disillusioned.

What Does the Church Really Need?

I don't believe that the church's greatest need is another sermon. We hear sermons all the time. Neither do we need to hear or sing a new worship song. Both are good and necessary, but we desperately need the discipline of obeying God and His Word. Obedience opens, disobedience shuts! We need to lay down our lives in prayer and help raise up others who will join us as we seek God's face, not just His hand.

If our heavens have become brass, we need to examine ourselves and say, "Have we disobeyed God and neglected to pray?" The *first thing* Jesus did when He entered His adult ministry at the age of 30 was to go away alone to a desert place, where He fasted and prayed!

Listen, my friend: If the Son of God felt the need to pray to the Father so fervently and unceasingly before He ministered, how can we justify our prayerless ways? We cannot. As we face severe opposition in these last days, it is evident that God is raising up prayer warriors and intercessors who will operate in divine revelation.

We saw fervent prayer and determined obedience blast holes in the heavens of brass over Pensacola, as well as other places in the United States and around the world. We saw the glory of God come suddenly under clear heavens and envelop thousands of worshipers in His weighty presence! Believe me, once you taste and see just how good the Lord's presence can be, you will never settle for second-best blessings under cloudy heavens of brass. Revival is available, but if you want it to come to you, your city, and your church, you must humble yourself and pray until an opening appears in the heavens of brass! It is time to see God's glory descend in all His incredible power and beauty. The world is waiting for the Church to get right with God—*submitting to Him* and resisting the devil.

Endnotes

1. See 1 Corinthians 13:1.
2. See 1 Samuel 4:21.
3. See Ephesians 6:12.
4. Deuteronomy 28:23.
5. See Ephesians 4:27.
6. See Galatians 3:7-9,14; 4:28.

CHAPTER 2

THE DEVIL TRAFFICS IN DRY PLACES

According to your holiness,
so shall be your success.
A holy man is an awesome
weapon in the hands of God.
—ROBERT MURRAY M'CHEYNE
(1813-1843)

The scene was chaotic when I drove up to the row of old Quonset huts on the Warner Robins Air Force Base in Georgia, where I pastored. I was asked to speak to a small group of workers on the base that day, but I remember the dogs most clearly. Several military police officers were trying to restrain some German Shepherds that looked like they had gone mad. They were growling, barking wildly, and straining with every muscle in their bodies to lunge toward a car that was parked near the officers. Suddenly, the senior officer looked toward the dogs and shouted out with a voice of command, "Heel!"

Instantly, those agitated dogs sat down on their haunches, and the restraining leashes went slack. The dogs were still quivering—with their ears erect, their eyes wide with excitement, and their mouths salivating in their eagerness to go—but they no longer jumped and pulled wildly.

As I witnessed this amazing transformation, I realized I was watching a canine drug detection unit going through a training exercise. These highly trained drug-sniffing dogs smelled the drugs the MPs had planted in a parked car, which was the cause of the dogs' agitation. However, this wasn't the point of the training exercise. The MPs already knew the dogs could smell the drugs because they had been created with that natural ability. The training exercise was designed to test their obedience, and the dogs had passed the test.

Obedience Is of Utmost Importance to God

Obedience means more to God than any set of gifts, abilities, or accomplishments. Compare Samson and Joseph for a moment. Both rose from obscurity to become deliverers of Israel. One used the supernatural strength in his body to rescue God's people; the other triumphed by depending entirely on God.

Samson and Joseph were also alike in that each faced sexual temptation at a crucial point in his life. Samson's life was put on the line when Delilah's flattering attention enticed him. Ignoring the direct command of God not to marry or fornicate with women who served other gods, Samson panted after Delilah and strained against God's command. He pursued his lust and lost God's supernatural strength.

In his time of temptation, Joseph completely resisted both his youthful lusts and the advances of Potiphar's seductive wife. Listening to the command of God, he immediately fled from this woman's grasp. In essence, Joseph "heeled" at God's command. He passed the test of obedience and was rewarded with a long life filled with God's provision and blessings. The purpose for which he had been born was safeguarded and released by his obedience.

On the other hand, Samson failed his test of obedience and suffered greatly at the hands of his enemies. Cruel treatment, blindness, and humiliation were Samson's lot as his enemies publicly mocked him. In the end, Samson redeemed himself and fulfilled his mission only by sacrificing his own life.

The lives of King Saul and King David also show the truth that obedience is of utmost importance to God. Saul was born with all the natural attributes of a king. By birth, he was a leader with a charismatic personality and countenance. Still, the river of God's glory did not flow in his life as it did in David's because Saul, like Samson, failed the test of obedience. He cared more for the praise of men than for the approval of God. Therefore, his life became one of the Bible's most potent symbols of rebellion against God. Nearly every Christian can quote the words Samuel spoke to Saul because of his disobedience.

> Behold, to obey is better than sacrifice and to hearken than the fat of rams. For rebellion is as the sin of witchcraft, and stubbornness is as iniquity and idolatry (1 Samuel 15:22-23).

King David carried the anointing under an open heaven to rule Israel. King Saul forfeited his anointing under a heaven of brass. King David ministered to Saul on the harp from the anointing that flowed from an open sky. On the other hand, King Saul desperately sought relief from his demons with no help from a clabbered sky. Saul's disobedience utterly closed the heavens over his head and drove him to a witch for counsel, eventually leading him to suicide and the destruction of his family line.

Some people may say, "Well, Pastor, that was then, and this is now." Do not forget that God does not change! He still hates iniquity and rebellion. Two things God talks about most in the Bible are obedience and disobedience. No matter how fast we talk, we will never be able to divert the Lord from this subject. Jesus was direct about His opinion of our excuses, justifications, and explanations for disobedience.

> *Many will say to me in that day, Lord, Lord, have we not prophesied in thy name? and in thy name have cast out devils? and in thy name done many wonderful works? And then will I profess unto them, I never knew you: depart from me, ye that work iniquity. ...And every one that heareth these sayings of mine, and doeth them not, shall be likened unto a foolish man, which built his house upon the sand* (Matthew 7:22-23,26).

Make no mistake about it: *The river of God will not flow in a bed of disobedience!* Sin causes the abundant river of the Spirit to dry up in our lives. It produces spiritual and natural drought and puts us in a perilous position.

Jesus was born under thickened skies, which had resisted the word of God for 400 long years. No prophet or preacher had spoken anointed words from Heaven for four centuries. By the time Jesus was born, the sin of rebellion had produced dry religion, captivity, poverty, widespread disease, and unchecked demonic activity.

You Will See Open Heavens

Before the Cross and the advent of the Holy Spirit on the earth, the atmosphere on this planet was so permeated with evil that no one today could begin to imagine what life was like under this stifling blanket. Solomon described the nightmare of life under thickened skies:

> *So I returned, and considered all the oppressions that are done under the sun: and* [I beheld] *the tears of such as were oppressed, and they had no comforter; and on the side of their oppressors there was power; but they had no comforter* (Ecclesiastes 4:1).

Solomon was the wisest man who ever lived except for Christ. Despite his wisdom, he was lamenting the fact that power was on the side of the oppressor—the people had no comforter and no power. Things were so bad during his lifetime that it was better that men not even be born! As bad as things may appear right now, our world is wonderful compared to Solomon's world.

God's Son, armed with a secret He could hardly wait to reveal to His oppressed followers, stepped right into the middle of this depressing picture of darkness, ignorance, and hopelessness. He knew that the world was about to change forever—a change He promised during His earthly ministry when He said God would send His people a *Comforter,* and they would receive *power!* With the coming of God's Spirit, men and women no longer have to live oppressed, suppressed, and depressed lives, as they did during Solomon's lifetime.

> *Jesus saw Nathanael coming to him, and saith of him, Behold an Israelite indeed, in whom is no guile! Nathanael saith unto him, Whence knowest thou me? Jesus answered and said unto him, Before that Philip called thee, when thou wast under the fig tree, I saw thee. Nathanael answered and saith unto him, Rabbi, thou art the Son of God; thou art the King of Israel. Jesus answered and said unto him, Because I said unto thee, I saw thee under the fig tree, believest thou? thou shall see greater things than these. And he saith unto him, Verily, verily, I say unto you, Hereafter ye shall see heaven open, and the angels of God ascending and descending upon the Son of man* (John 1:47-51).

When skies are overcast, the clouds have no power to separate you from the Lord. Even on a clear day when the sky is bright blue, a casual glance tells you there is nothing between you and space. When Jesus told Nathaniel, "*You shall see heaven open,*" He referred to a heaven that is not rooted in the natural realm. He talked about the heaven that can harden and thicken through widespread disobedience. When Jesus told Nathanael that he would see heaven open, He was saying Nathanael would be an eyewitness to His victorious life of obedience. Even under hopelessly thickened clouds of brass, Nathanael would see the fruit of total obedience.

Jesus wasn't interested in becoming the main attraction of a big conference. He didn't seek popularity and didn't expect the title of "Rabboni" or "great teacher." He wanted to touch us right where we live. He wanted to obey His Father and see His disciples follow in His footsteps.

Jesus was fully God and fully man, but He didn't draw on His deity to overcome the world, the flesh, or the devil. He overcame it all as an anointed *man* because He knew that was how *you and I* would have to overcome our obstacles. Otherwise, it would have been totally unfair for Him to say, "Follow Me."[2] He could have shown His omnipotence, omniscience, and omnipresence on earth because He was, after all, the Son of God. Instead, He chose not to move in these divine powers so He could legally invade the realm of the flesh as a man. Referring to Himself as the Son of Man, He pointedly emphasized His birth through the obedience of a very human mother and showed us how to live as a man who perfectly obeyed His Father.

1. Jesus did not move in omnipotence on earth.

He was obedient and dependent.

> *The Son can do nothing of himself, but what he seeth the Father do: for what things soever he doeth, these also doeth the Son likewise* (John 5:19b).

2. *Jesus did not move in omniscience on earth.*

He told His disciples concerning His second coming:

> *But of that day and that hour knoweth no man, no,*
> *not the angels which are in heaven, neither the Son,*
> *but the Father* (Mark 13:32).

The things He learned, He discovered the old-fashioned way—through prayer, the study of Scriptures, and long hours communing with God the Father. Had Jesus been omniscient, He would have known when He would be returning.

3. *Jesus was not omnipresent while on earth.*

> *Then said Martha unto Jesus, Lord, if thou hadst*
> *been here, my brother had not died* (John 11:21).

Jesus could be in only one place at a time because He was not omnipresent. Therefore, He said:

> *It is expedient for you that I go away* (John 16:7).

God is always interested in the fruit of our lives—the fruit of obedience. Nearly every book in the Bible speaks of the effects of God's presence in the lives of men and women. The parable of the talents is about fruit.[3] Likewise, the Book of Revelation is about fruit. Every time Jesus spoke to one of the seven churches through the prophecy of John, He commended them for their godly fruit or chastised them for their lack of fruit. Using the phrase "to him who overcomes," Jesus showed each church the benefits of obedience and perseverance.

Ephesus

To him that overcometh will I give to eat of the tree of life, which is in the midst of the paradise of God (Revelation 2:7b).

Smyrna

He that overcometh shall not be hurt of the second death (Revelation 2:11b).

Pergamos

To him that overcometh will I give to eat of the hidden manna, and will give him a white stone, and in the stone a new name written, which no man knoweth saving he that receiveth it (Revelation 2:17b).

Thyatira

And he that overcometh, and keepeth my works unto the end, to him will I give power over the nations: and he shall rule them with a rod of iron; as the vessels of a potter shall they be broken to shivers: even as I received of my Father. And I will give him the morning star (Revelation 2:26-28).

Sardis

He that overcometh, the same shall be clothed in white raiment; and I will not blot out his name out of the book of life, but I will confess his name before my Father, and before his angels (Revelation 3:5).

Philadelphia

Him that overcometh will I make a pillar in the temple of my God, and he shall go no more out: and I will write upon him the name of my God, and the name of the city of my God, which is new Jerusalem, which cometh down out of heaven from my God: and I will write upon him my new name (Revelation 3:12).

Laodicea

To him that overcometh will I grant to sit with me in my throne, even as I also overcame, and am set down with my Father in his throne (Revelation 3:21).

God has never lifted His requirement that we must overcome sin and the devil. If Jesus told every church in the Book of Revelation to overcome, it is important to God that we overcome as well! To each of us, He says, *"to him that overcometh"* not "to him who muddles his way through in failure, selfishness, and foolishness."

Obedience Opens the Heavens

The fruit of obedience is the privilege of seeing the heavens open. Obedience to God always produces a supernatural flow of His anointing and ensures His will is done on earth as in Heaven.

Nathanael walked, talked, and shared meals and ministry with Jesus for over three years. With his own eyes, he watched the Master put the devil to flight. He saw fear banished, blind eyes opened, and the lame walk. He saw lifelong captives freed from demon possession, physical affliction, and spiritual oppression.

Today, we have the living Spirit of God dwelling within us. We have the wealth of God's Word, as well as the ability to read the Scriptures ourselves. We have the name of Jesus and the authority of His shed blood in our arsenal of spiritual weapons.

We cannot get religious and stick these things into some "nice Bible story" category. God will come through every time you obey Him, just like He did for Jesus Christ. That is the point of the Lord's promise to Nathanael. If you walk like Jesus walked—and remember, He did it all as a *man* who did not pull from any resource other than those available to man—you too will see heaven open over your life! No matter how thick the heavens over your city or region might be, this is true. Jesus never meant for the miraculous life to be limited only to Himself. He ordained that you and I should walk in the miraculous too! He was the prototype of many to come after Him, the firstborn of many sons.

> *And these signs shall follow them that believe; In my name shall they cast out devils; they shall speak with new tongues; they shall take up serpents; and if they drink any deadly thing, it shall not hurt them; they shall lay hands on the sick, and they shall recover* (Mark 16:17-18).

Satan Traffics in Dry Places

Disobedience does more than cause the skies to thicken over our heads. According to God's warning in the Book of Deuteronomy, disobedience also causes the earth under our feet to become iron.[4] Iron equates to dryness, drought, and famine. It is in the arid land that the devil begins to roam.

> *When the unclean spirit is gone out of a man, he walketh through dry places, seeking rest, and findeth none* (Matthew 12:43).

The evil one traffics in dry places because he cannot co-exist with the manifest presence of the river of God. Any area of our lives that lacks the life-giving flow of God's Spirit is ripe for occupation by our most spiteful enemy.

The sin of disobedience steals our health and robs us of the ability to prosper. It brings pain to our path and bruises our feet with cruel, cold hardness. It produces thick darkness and cuts off our productivity, prosperity, and means of survival. It breeds guilt and causes us to be difficult to live with because it separates us from God and puts a wedge between other believers and us.

Think about the times you have disobeyed God. I am sure that no one had to tell you when the heavens over your head were hardening. You knew that something had come between you and the Lord! If you do not repent and remove the sin that separates you from God, the heavens become brass, and you eventually *suffer*. Your family suffers, your friends suffer, and even your church suffers. Long before the clouds begin to gather over your head, the Spirit within gives you a clear sense that things are not right. You know it, your wife knows it, your children know it, and even the unsaved people around you know it. But the truth is that none of them can do anything about it. Repentance is a job that only you can do.

God said through the psalmist that the one who keeps His Word *"shall be like a tree planted by the rivers of water, that bringeth forth his fruit in his season; his leaf also shall not wither; and whatsoever he doeth shall prosper."*[5] This means that even if a drought strikes where you live, you will prosper because you are planted by the river of God!

The devil is powerless when you walk in unbroken fellowship with the Lord. He may have the *ability*, but he does not have the *authority* to do evil unless you give it to him. If you are obedient to the call of Christ Jesus, the minions of hell will recognize you! Keep yourself strong in the Spirit by feeding on God's Word, meditating on His precepts, and by testing the conditions of the heavens over your head. True, the devil will continue to try and harass, buffet, and hinder you in your attempt to draw near to God. However, he cannot harm you if the heavens are clear and open between you and God! Prayer, coupled with obedience, is the only way you can keep the heavens clear.

The Smallest Piece of the Pie

If you diagram the time spent in worship services each week in a typical congregation, prayer is the smallest piece of the pie. Announcements are given more time. Auxiliary activities are given more time. The receiving of tithes and offerings is given more time. Music is given more time. Preaching is given more time. The smallest slice of the pie is always given to prayer.

This is true not only for worship services but also for the church's activities. For example, a crowd will attend if you call a meeting for almost anything other than prayer. On the other hand, a prayer meeting will attract only a handful of people.

How sad! We must refocus our hearts and redirect our energies. Jesus said:

> *My house shall be called a house of prayer* (Matthew 21:13).

We have most certainly forgotten this. Our erroneous, man-made priorities have misled us. If we come into God's house and pursue His desires, much more time will be spent in prayer. As we do warfare, press in, and punch holes through heavens of brass, Satan will hold no power over our lives and churches. We suffer the effects of his presence until then, and the heavens over our heads become brass.

Endnotes

1. See John 14:26; Acts 1:8.
2. See Matthew 4:19.
3. See Matthew 25:14-30.
4. See Deuteronomy 28:23.
5. Psalm 1:3.

CHAPTER 3

EIGHT OBSTACLES TO BRASS-SHATTERING PRAYER

A friend gave me a simplified version of how cancer invades bodies. He said researchers report that after we are born, we have the potential for cancer cells to develop, especially if it runs in the family line. In fact, new potential cancer cells continue to appear until the day we die. Why then doesn't everyone get cancer? God endowed us with an immune system that destroys cancer cells with 100-percent efficiency and no side effects—until something weakens or compromises it. (This is grossly simplifying a very complex process.)

The prevailing medical theory is that we experience a breakdown in our natural defenses allowing damaged cells to multiply and become cancer cells. Therefore, the medical research community devotes much time to studying the human immune system. Researchers hope to discover a way to repair broken immune systems in cancer patients and stimulate their natural defense mechanisms so that cancer cells cannot multiply. The human immune system is nature's most effective anti-cancer treatment. Preventing the immune system from breaking down in the first place is the key to winning the war with cancer.

Types of Cells in Our Physical Bodies

As my friend and I talked more about the workings of the human body, he explained that at the heart of every cell is a minute strand of DNA. This is our genetic fingerprint, and each of us has a DNA print that is uniquely ours. It is the heart and mind of every cell in our bodies, including those in our fingernails, hair, skin, body organs, and blood. A normal, healthy human cell has a complete and unaltered DNA strand that contains all the information the cell will ever need for development and function. Each time a cell multiplies and creates new cells, it passes on that information.

The Healthy Cell

A healthy cell consumes energy, occupies space, and performs a specific task in perfect harmony with neighboring cells. Several cells follow specific DNA instructions to group together with other cells and perform specialized tasks. These cell groups form vital organs such as the liver, kidneys, heart, brain, lungs, and skin. Although these cells have special functions, they all contain the same central DNA code as every other cell in the individual's body.

The "Out-of-Place" Cell

Cells that are part of a second category seem to have lost their proper place in the body. These cells have the same primary DNA code as other cells, but they either missed the directions or just ignored them. Like healthy cells, they consume energy and occupy space, but they don't seem to belong anywhere and don't perform any functions or work in the body.

(If you are starting to feel uncomfortable, you are beginning to see how closely this describes the Body of Christ.) These cells gather in makeshift structures like moles, cysts, harmless growths (benign tumors), or other odd multiple-cell formations that don't have any particular purpose.

These freeloaders don't cause any trouble most of the time—they are just a nuisance. If they grow too much, they begin to impede the function of the working cells and organs. Some of these cells are especially sensitive. If on the skin, they are prone to be bumped, scraped, scratched, and irritated.

The Malignant Destroyer Cell

The third category of cells comes into existence when a DNA strand is damaged or altered. These cells start as benign cells whose DNA mutates because of outside influences. They consume energy at an elevated rate, with an excessive hunger for fuel. Sometimes they occupy too much space since they multiply quickly and constantly encroach on nearby cells and organs.

The most dangerous aspect of these cells is that they are greedy, demanding, unscrupulous, and merciless in their constant drive to satisfy their raging hunger. These cells are *malignant.* Perhaps their most dreaded characteristic is their ability to metastasize or migrate from one part of the body to another. With what appears to be peculiar and evil cunning, these cells constantly adapt and mutate so that they can cross barriers, infiltrate existing organs, build resistance to medical treatments, and consume nearby healthy cells. In general terms, these cells are corrupt; if left unchecked, they will ultimately destroy the life of their host. This third class of cells constitutes the vast legion of related diseases we call cancer. It can strike any living cell in the human body, which explains why there are many types of cancer.

The Natural Realm Reflects the Spiritual Realm

Just as there are three categories of cells in our physical bodies, so are there three classes of people in a body of believers. Initially, people are born into this world with the Ten Commandments indelibly stamped on their hearts. They are also born with a sinful nature inherited from Adam, their earthly ancestor. If left unchecked, this cancerous nature of sin threatens their existence. Rebirth through the blood of Christ, the second Adam, purifies their spiritual DNA and gives them the heart of God our Father.

The Healthy Believer

Healthy believers perform tasks of service in perfect harmony with other believers. Under specific instructions from their spiritual DNA strand, some Christians will group with other Christians for specialized functions within the Body. Yet all, from the pastor to the greeter, share a common spiritual DNA code that is unique—all share a link with one Head, Jesus Christ.

The "Out-of-Place" Believer

Every church also seems to have another group of believers who have good hearts but don't know their place or function in the local body. They are easy to spot because they never do any work in the church. They are primarily interested in being fed and sitting in their usual place where they can see and be seen by those coming and going. They are especially sensitive and resistant to change, so they are quick to complain when the sanctuary is too hot or cold, if the sermon goes too long, or if the preacher is "meddling." These believers are also slow to join in the congregation's work and serve the larger community. They consume a higher level of the ministry staff's time and energy than believers who actively serve the Lord. Given their inactivity, the second class of believers talks more than most. This often transforms and moves them into the third class of churchgoers.

The Malignant, Devouring Believer

People in the third class of believers have allowed chronic unforgiveness to turn into bitterness, which has mutated their spiritual DNA. Once the heart of a believer has been reconfigured by bitterness, they find it difficult to identify with other members of the Body. Thus, they are no longer content merely to occupy space and be fed but become hungry for more recognition, power, and influence in the church's operation. They begin to use their words and persuasion to press their will upon others and consume those who refuse to move to their beat. The root of bitterness has given Satan a place in their hearts, and their function has become destructive. To the outward eye, they are still sheep; but to the discerning eye of the Spirit, they have become devouring wolves. They have become cancer and a blight with a cunning determination to bring division and strife to the Body of Christ.

Prayer: God's Prescription for a Healthy Church Body

God designed the Body of Christ with a perfect system to deal with unforgiveness and bitterness long before serious problems arise. Spiritual cancer sets in when God's people do not follow His plan for a healthy spiritual life and allow the Body's built-in defenses to fail. These failures are almost always traceable to the congregation's failure to pray and follow God's Word. By definition, God's house is a house of prayer.[1] It is logical to say that if a church doesn't pray, it has no right to call itself God's house. One thing is sure: Spiritual cancer is on the way if a church doesn't pray.

Drink of the Spirit Daily for Total Spiritual Health

Another brief example from the natural realm will help us better understand prayer's role in the spiritual realm and revival. A healthy human body can go for up to 40 days without food before serious, life-threatening complications set in. At the end of the first day of a fast, the individual may experience weakness, slight disorientation, headaches, or energy loss, but they will survive. However, doctors say that the human body cannot safely go without water for more than three days. After that point, anyone who has not drunk water risks permanent damage to major organs, which leads to imminent death as organs begin to fail.

Similarly, the life of our spirit-man is nurtured as we feed on God's Word and drink of His Spirit. You may squeak by in your Christian life without reading and meditating on God's Word for some time. However, if you try to wander through life without regularly drinking from His Spirit in prayer and communion, you risk a severe attack on the most treasured and vital parts of your existence! A body separated from its head is a corpse! Prayer is the drink and life-sustaining breath of the believer as well as the Church. If prayer is absent, serious impairment or death is near. I believe God will bring revival to America to save her life! Revival is God's intensive care unit as He connects to His Body with a massive influx of oxygen and life-giving fluids! The breath and river of God revive the life of the Church, but God's desire is for us to begin drawing breath and seeking His Spirit without outside assistance!

Fervent prayer is crucial for our survival, and we know it. Someone else also knows this. The adversary trembles every time he overhears a blood-washed saint committing to pray. We may be blind to the truth, but the devil is not. He knows the real power of prayer in the life of a submitted saint and fears the fires ignited by Spirit-led intercession. Therefore, he will do almost anything to keep God's people from praying.

The Adversary's Plan of Attack

The moment you step into a private place for prayer, every possible diversion, task, amusement, or offense will come to mind and present itself as an emergency. You wouldn't let any of these things pull you away from your favorite television program or hobby, but in the prayer closet, they seem to take on immense importance. When you kneel to pray, push aside every hindrance that the devil drops into your thoughts and fulfill your intention to pray.

In addition to hindrances the enemy concocts to stop our prayers, we carry other obstacles into the prayer closet with us. These obstacles must be addressed if we desire to prevail in prayer and pierce the thickened skies over our heads.

Obstacle #1: Unforgiveness: Brass-shattering prayer will not flow through unforgiving hearts.

Because unforgiveness quickly turns into bitterness, it is the first and perhaps the most serious blockage to fervent, effectual prayer. Jesus taught His disciples much about the relationship between unforgiveness and prayer.

> *Therefore if thou bring thy gift to the altar, and there rememberest that thy brother hath ought against thee; leave there thy gift before the altar, and go thy way; first be reconciled to thy brother, and then come and offer thy gift* (Matthew 5:23-24).
>
> *After this manner therefore pray ye: ...And forgive us our debts, as we forgive our debtors. ...But if ye forgive not men their trespasses, neither will your Father forgive your trespasses* (Matthew 6:9a, 12,15).
>
> *And when ye stand praying, forgive, if ye have ought against any: that your Father also which is in heaven may forgive you your trespasses* (Mark 11:25).

The apostle Paul warned of another consequence of unforgiveness when he told the believers at Corinth:

To whom ye forgive any thing, I forgive also: for if I forgave any thing, to whom I forgave it, for your sakes forgave I it in the person of Christ; lest Satan should get an advantage of us: for we are not ignorant of his devices (2 Corinthians 2:10-11).

Unforgiveness Mimics Multiple Sclerosis

In further discussions with my friend mentioned earlier, he said that unforgiveness strikes at the heart of our communication lines with God, much like multiple sclerosis attacks the human spinal cord and central nervous system. The Bible says:

Hatred stirreth up strifes: but love covereth all sins (Proverbs 10:12).

Love is the supernatural covering that protects, heals, and shields the Body of Christ from internal strife and injury. In the human body, a myelin sheath protects the countless nerves that are bundled together in the spinal cord, much like plastic or rubber insulation shields electrical wires from shorting out against other wires or conductive substances like water.

When the Body Devours Itself

During our discussion about unforgiveness, my friend noted that researchers think the disease of multiple sclerosis somehow causes its victim's immune system to turn against their body. The immune system begins to attack the myelin sheath as if it were an unwanted intruder. Each attack leaves scars on the delicate spinal cord ("sclerosis" means "scarring") until these assaults gradually begin to perforate this protective barrier. When the damage becomes severe, it causes the nerves in the spinal cord to short out like a telephone cable that has accidentally been severed. This hinders or destroys direct communication between the head and the body, causing weakness, partial paralysis, and other symptoms.

Unforgiveness Short-Circuits Prayer

Unforgiveness strikes directly at our prayer cord, a vital link to our Redeemer. It cuts us off from God's forgiveness and authorizes Satan to begin thickening the skies over our heads. It is a serious sin because it causes us to withdraw from another believer, causing separation from God's life-giving flow. Any extremity or organ in the human body that is cut off from the life-giving flow of blood begins to atrophy and eventually die.

When we first repent, we correctly acknowledge that Jesus forgives us for our sins. However, when we hold unforgiveness in our hearts, even toward people who wronged us before we became believers, that unforgiveness becomes a weight that hinders our faith and disarms us of our power to pray with assurance and confidence. There is no offense worth the separation from God that we experience when we harbor unforgiveness.

Releasing the people who have harmed and inflicted unbearable pain on us will release us to progress in God's plan. It will free our faith to see prayers catapult heavenward every time we pray. Unforgiveness is hazardous to your health. It does not pay to hold a grudge. Be slow to anger and quick to forgive! Unforgiveness is also material that thickens the heavens over your head. Out of all Ten Commandments, six deal with people-to-people (horizontal) communication, and four deal with people-to-God (vertical) communication. God knew we would have conflicts with each other. That is why He gave us more commandments concerning our horizontal relationships than our relationship with Him.

Obstacle #2: Regarding Iniquity: Iniquity destroys the power of brass-shattering prayer.

Eli, the priest, will be forever remembered for two reasons. First, God used him to train Samuel from his early years to adulthood. Samuel was destined to become one of God's greatest prophets. He would anoint Saul, Israel's first king, and David, Israel's greatest king.

Second, Eli raised two worthless sons who are among the most despised men in the entire Bible! Ultimately, God brought judgment on Eli's house because he *regarded iniquity* by looking the other way while his sons made a mockery of the temple and the sacrifices offered there. These men were committing adultery with women right in the temple, and Eli failed to correct and discipline them. Finally, God did what Eli would not do. Not only did God stop the blatant iniquity of Eli's sons, but He also cut off the entire family line. Eli's wicked sons were both struck down. The hated Philistines captured the ark of God, and Eli fell and broke his neck when he heard the news. Thus, Eli's family line came to a bitter end.[2]

The story of Eli should be a chilling warning to parents of every generation. We should never try to cover up or condone the sins of our children. God knows what they are doing, and He also sees our failure to correct them! He cannot be hoodwinked or distracted from the actual spiritual condition of our lives.

David wrote in the Psalms:

If I regard, iniquity in my heart, the Lord will not hear me: (Psalm 66:18)

Today we might say, "If I cherish lawlessness or sin in my heart, the Lord will not hear my prayers." King Saul cherished the praises of the people more than the approval of God. When confronted by the prophet of God, he cherished his reputation more than the truth and blamed his people for something he had done. Even after he realized David had been chosen by God Himself to assume the throne of Israel, Saul vainly tried to kill God's chosen man for many years.

The Hebrew word for *regard* in this verse is *ra'ah*. Among other things, it means "to gaze, to look joyfully, to enjoy or experience a thing."[3] Don't go into your prayer closet and expect to see the glory of God if you have been gazing upon and enjoying sin in another room! Too many Christian homes have become contaminated by sexually explicit movies, television programs, and other media that scornfully ridicule moral principles and godly living. Every time you feed on such things, you are literally regarding iniquity in your heart! Another meaning of *ra'ah* is "to spy and stare."[4] Don't grab your smartphone, hide in the bathroom, and resort to surfing the internet for pornographic thrills. You are spying on forbidden fruit when you look at a woman other than your wife and allow your mind to fantasize. Sin occurs in the mind and heart, even if your body never gets involved. Repent of any sin, renounce any return to that sin, and get back to holiness.

Another way we regard iniquity involves the people we respect, honor, or look up to. (Don't act religious—I know you have your heroes too.) God is far more interested in a man's inner character than in his outward appearance and performance. You need to repent if you catch yourself idolizing an athlete, politician, actor, or actress. You have regarded iniquity in your heart. The Scriptures warn us:

> *Keep thy heart with all diligence; for out of it are the issues of life* (Proverbs 4:23).

Guard your heart, and don't let iniquity find a home in your life or affections.

A lax attitude toward sin also amounts to a lax attitude toward iniquity. James, the apostle, warned the Church about the dangers of friendship with the world and its effect on prayer:

> *Ye ask, and receive not, because ye ask amiss, that ye may consume it upon your lusts. Ye adulterers and adulteresses, know ye not that the friendship of the world is enmity with God? whosoever therefore will be a friend of the world is the enemy of God* (James 4:3-4).

We regard iniquity in our hearts when we cling to a position we know is unrighteous. Often, we insist on justifying our actions or opinions at any cost because we don't want to admit we are wrong. This is pride. When pride lurks in the shadows, motivating this kind of attitude, it must be cast down. If pride could make a devil out of an archangel, what might it do to you? You may think you can get by, but think again!

You embrace and endorse a lie when you refuse to accept the truth. Who gets the honor and glory for this kind of foolishness—God or the devil? Whose kingdom is built and strengthened? Who is most pleased when you promote a lie to cling to a *cherished* position? Remember, the river of God will never flow through a bed of disobedience. Cast away the lie, release your pride, and cling to that which is good and true. Then the power of God can and will flow through you again.

Obstacle #3: Prejudice: When prejudice is truly done away with, skies of brass shatter.

A woman dying in a hospital called her pastor and asked for prayer. This godly pastor understood that the Holy Spirit distributes His supernatural gifts "severally as He wills"[5] among the members of His Body. So he asked a particular African American man in the church, who operated powerfully in the gift of healing, to go to the hospital and pray for the desperately ill woman.

The woman's face lit up in anticipation when she saw the door to her hospital room open. She knew the pastor was sending someone from the church to pray for her healing, and she was hoping for a miracle. When the door swung open, and she realized that her visitor was a black man, she instantly said, "No! You will *not* lay hands on me!" So insistent was she that the only thing the dismayed man could do was turn and leave. The woman's condition kept getting worse until the doctors finally moved her to the intensive care unit in hopes of somehow keeping her alive. No treatment appeared to be working.

Finally, the woman realized her end was near if God didn't intervene. She was so weak that she could barely speak above a whisper, but she managed to raise her finger and attract a nurse's attention. When the nurse stepped closer and bent down, she heard the woman weakly whisper, "Please call my pastor again. Tell him he can send anyone to pray for me, including the black man. If I don't get a miracle, I'm going to die." The black brother returned to the hospital, but this time he stood at the woman's bedside, laid his hands on her, and offered a powerful prayer for her healing. God raised up the woman from her deathbed that day and made her whole.

The Holy Spirit divides His gifts among whomsoever He wills. Sometimes, He gives the gift you need to someone you can't tolerate. Sooner or later, you will have to make amends with this person to receive what you need.

God, our Father, is determined to conform us into the image of His Son, which involves much change and transformation. Sometimes this means that we must let go of prejudices and notions.

In this story, the African American man possessed the gift that would bring the woman healing. God was ready to heal her at any time, but the woman was not ready to accept God's gift from that man. Only when the doctors' prescriptions and treatments didn't work, and she was facing imminent death, was she willing to ask the Lord for healing and accept His plan. All along, God had the prescription the dying woman needed, but first He required her to release a prejudice that had a death grip on her life. The woman, however, felt justified in clinging to her racial prejudice even while she confessed Jesus Christ as her Lord. She refused to believe that God would bring her healing through hands of a different skin color than her own. Once she yielded to the will of God, He saved her life through the gifts, faith, and anointed prayers of the same African American brother she had once rejected. When she released her prejudice, God released her healing. What will He require you to release before He brings revival to your life or church?

Most of the problems Paul the apostle encountered were rooted in racial and religious prejudice. This was also the root of almost every major problem in the early Church. In each case, prejudice threatened to divide the brethren and nullify the mystery of the Gospel. While God honored the Jews, the descendants of Abraham, He was careful to include people from many other nations and races in the genealogy of the Messiah. He planned to bring all nations into His Kingdom under one blood, banner, and Savior, Jesus Christ.

Paul constantly battled against the religious prejudice of Jews against all non-Jewish converts to Christ, but he struck a blow against almost every form of prejudice when he told the churches:

> There is neither Jew nor Greek, there is neither bond nor free, there is neither male nor female: for ye are all one in Christ Jesus. And if ye be Christ's, then are ye Abraham's seed, and heirs according to the promise (Galatians 3:28-29).

Paul leaves no room for racial prejudice, gender prejudice, or occupational or economic prejudice! In God's presence, all men and women share one common status—we are all sinners saved by grace and grace alone. It is by God's grace that we are saved. It is by His grace that we dwell together in unity. Everyone has access to the presence of God through the name of Jesus and the power of His shed blood. If we insist on clinging to our prejudices, we are failing to recognize the true Body of Christ. This is an affront to God.

> *For by one Spirit are we all baptized into one body, whether we be Jews or Gentiles, whether we be bond or free; and have been all made to drink into one Spirit. For the body is not one member, but many. ...But now hath God set the members every one of them in the body, as it hath pleased him. ...And the eye cannot say unto the hand, I have no need of thee: nor again the head to the feet, I have no need of you. ...That there should be no schism in the body; but that the members should have the same care one for another* (1 Corinthians 12:13-14,18,21,25).

For many generations, numerous American churches preached and acted as if one gospel was for the white man and another for the black man. Every time Galatians 3:28-29 was read in their meetings, it was followed by a resounding "but" and some dubious justification for condoning prejudice. Any time you catch yourself saying, "Yes, but..." when reading the Word of God, ask yourself why you are "butting" your head against God! Somebody is in error, and it isn't God.

People have held to their prejudices and opinions so stubbornly that blood has been shed, and thousands of people have died needlessly. Obedience to God's Word would have saved nations from the unspeakable sorrow and heartbreak they endured through conflict.

Prejudice inflicts misery and strife on people of nearly every continent of the world and has spawned countless bloody wars and conflicts. Almost every tyrant who imprisoned and overpowered other nations was propelled into power by the sheer force of hatred and prejudice. One mark of *true revival* is that it gathers all people under the Son, bridging the chasms that separate races, genders, and the world's many social and ethnic groups.

Obstacle #4: Judgment of Others: A heart that judges dilutes the force of the prayers intended to break through brass.

Judgmentalism is another sin that blocks or hinders our prayers. Jesus warned His disciples and all who would trust in Him:

> *Judge not, that ye be not judged. For with what judgment ye judge, ye shall be judged: and with what measure ye mete, it shall be measured to you again. And why beholdest thou the mote that is in thy brother's eye, but considerest not the beam that is in thine own eye? Or how wilt thou say to thy brother, Let me pull out the mote out of thine eye; and, behold, a beam is in thine own eye? Thou hypocrite, first cast out the beam out of thine own*

eye; and then shall thou see clearly to cast out the mote out of thy brother's eye (Matthew 7:1-5).

He also told a hostile crowd of religious leaders:

Judge not according to the appearance, but judge righteous judgment (John 7:24).

You may occasionally have to judge the fruits of righteousness in a person's life, but that doesn't mean God has called you to a new career as a "holy fruit inspector." That is nothing more than a fancy name for gossiping and self-righteous hypocrisy. Follow the counsel of Jesus: Judge not so you won't be judged.

We love to judge and compare others to ourselves, the best example of godliness we know. We like to compare the doctrines of others to the most accurate doctrine we know—ours. We delight in judging their children, clothing, careers, and spouses, hoping to find they are far inferior to ours. We scrutinize one another's vacations, cars, furniture, and homes. We land self-righteous judgments on pastors, including their teaching, preaching, and things their wives try to do. All the while, we are building our apparent goodness and trying to affirm our favor with God and man. We have the uncanny ability to see ourselves as more gifted, better equipped, and more compassionate than most anyone else.

Most of us know better than to outright brag. Instead, we express our superiority in genuine-sounding concerns about the less fortunate in our churches or workplaces. "Thank God we are there to fill the gap when all these lesser life forms fail" is our attitude. This nonsense is the standard operating procedure in churches all over the world. It keeps the heavens brass and prevents true intercession from rising in our hearts unto the Lord.

Administering a Spiritual Forensics Test

I wonder how many people "sleep before their time"? What would happen if we exhumed them from their graves and ran a spiritual forensics test? We might find that physical disease had nothing to do with their untimely deaths! We might discover that they died from the spiritual disease of judgmentalism and their refusal to accept those they disliked as joint members in the Body of Christ. Paul, the apostle, was blunt when he wrote to the Corinthians about properly observing communion.

> *For he that eateth and drinketh unworthily, eateth and drinketh damnation to himself, not discerning the Lord's body. For this cause many are weak and sickly among you, and many sleep. For if we would judge ourselves, we should not be judged* (1 Corinthians 11:29-31).

Bitterness, unforgiveness, and prejudice can all manifest as judgmentalism that wrongfully excludes people from God's Kingdom. When we judge others, we bring God's judgment on our own heads. (It is also possible that some children have cut short their lives because they failed to honor their parents in childhood and later as adults.)

The cure is simple—let Jesus be your plumb line! This sobering appraisal will most certainly silence the hypocrite within. Jesus commanded this personal introspection when He told the crowd, which was about to stone the woman caught in adultery, *"He that is without sin among you, let him first cast a stone at her."*[6]

Indeed, our Lord knows us better than we know ourselves. He admonishes us:

> *And if the blind lead the blind, both shall fall into the ditch* (Matthew 15:14b).

He warned us of the arrogance of assuming we know better than others. Paul gave us similar advice when he said:

> *But they measuring themselves by themselves, and comparing themselves among themselves, are not wise* (2 Corinthians 10:12b).

When God moves in revival, He often shows people a picture of themselves, an image they rarely see. This supernatural shock treatment usually leads to repentance. David said:

> *I thought on my ways, and turned my feet unto thy testimonies. I made haste, and delayed not to keep thy commandments* (Psalm 119:59-60).

The only ones throwing accusations at believers should be the devil and his minions. God expects that kind of language to come from them. Satan is called the *"accuser of the brethren."*[7] His punishment is already decreed in the Bible. If you are critical of others and your mouth spews out degrading comments and accusations, I think you should ask yourself, *"Which master am I serving with my thoughts and words?"* You may need to be delivered from a critical spirit. If you devour others with your words, you are yielding your tongue to evil. Stop judging, repent, and you will see heavens of brass shatter!

Obstacle #5: Ignoring the Poor: When you open your heart to the needy, God opens the heavens to you.

One of the most stinging accusations leveled today is that the Church has abandoned the poor and needy to the government. It stings because it is true. No matter what the federal government has done in the past or plans to do in the future, God has not suspended or revoked our obligation to care for the poor! Solomon warned:

> *Whoso stoppeth his ears at the cry of the poor, he also shall cry himself, but shall not be heard* (Proverbs 21:13).

This is a sobering statement. I don't know about you, but I never want to be in a situation where God will not hear my cry.

In the Book of Acts, one of the first major conflicts in the new church at Jerusalem involved its ministry to needy widows and orphans. That conflict might not occur in some churches today, but that is not something to brag about. Most churches don't provide care for our widows and orphans, causing them to be dumped into the unloving arms of governmental welfare agencies and the weary arms of overloaded benevolent organizations.

On an individual level, most Christians are insulated from contact with the poor and don't even know *how* to reach out to the needy! We know almost nothing about the daily struggles of the homeless and are not even sure we want to know. If we think about the lonely and sometimes desperate lives elderly widows often lead, we quickly dismiss such unhappy thoughts and ponder less disturbing subjects. We may just shake our heads and say, "Oh my, that's such a shame," when we see a child who has lost one or both parents to accidents, war, or sickness, but our compassion most often stops right there. Instead of reaching out to that unfortunate child, we are happy to go back home to the safety of our cocoon, far from the crying needs of the poor and destitute.

There is a reason we feel so touched when we meet a needy person. The Spirit of God within us rouses our sleepy senses and urges us to action. Every Scripture we have read about caring for the hurting assails us with fresh imagery, and the stereotypes we have crafted about the poor shame us as they fall to the ground. Suddenly, we realize that the poor are simply people who need more than they currently have. They are struggling to survive. If Jesus walked the earth today, we would more likely find Him with the poor than inside our church doors.

Look again at the Scripture in Proverbs 21:13:

Whoso stoppeth his ears at the cry of the poor, he also shall cry himself, but shall not be heard.

What a powerful Scripture. How we treat the poor has a vital impact on whether we are heard by others or God!

God describes the poor in many ways and always with compassion. Although the Lord doesn't expect us to cast away all else and make the care of the poor our only priority, He does expect us to heed the cries of the poor when He leads them into our path. Jesus ministered only to those His Father chose, even if it meant most people in a crowd did not receive healing or deliverance. At other times, He ministered to all:

> *Now when the sun was setting, all they that had any sick with divers diseases brought them unto him; and he laid his hands on every one of them, and healed them* (Luke 4:40).

Most churches are geared to provide a one-time gift of cash, clothing, or food to tide poor people over. The problem is that many impoverished people can't be helped merely by a single handout. Like our Master, we must walk among them, comfort them, eat meals with them, and minister to them before lasting results are seen. Some individuals can be rescued from poverty through the regeneration of their spirits and the renewal of their minds with the Word of God. Others need tangible aid in addition to the regeneration since their earthly source of income has been lost through death, disease, or other unfortunate circumstances. The Church needs to help shoulder the responsibility of providing for their needs. This was how the church in Jerusalem was ministering to the widows and orphans in their midst.

The revived Church is a caring Church. The revived believer is a serving believer.

Obstacle #6: Teaching the Commandments of Men: When we are willing to turn from the precepts of men, we see the commandments of God breaking through cloudy skies.

Many believers around the country pray ineffectively and live in continual frustration and discouragement because they have believed the commandments of men rather than the doctrines of God.

> *This people draweth nigh unto me with their mouth, and honoureth me with their lips; but their heart is far from me. But in vain they do worship me, teaching far doctrines the commandments of men* (Matthew 15:8-9).

Many of the commandments represented in our churches as doctrines virtually require Christians to disallow or recast the Word of God as revealed in the New Testament. Anxious Bible teachers and preachers scramble to reassure their audiences that many things passed away with the apostles—which they did not—as if they were *limited* to the ministry of the apostles. It seems that anything relating to a *supernatural God* who does *supernatural works* in our day is systematically purged to conform with the tidy commandments of men.

In many Charismatic and Pentecostal churches, ministers disregard certain Bible verses seemingly in conflict with their favorite man-made doctrines. The God of revival cares nothing for the commandments of men, but He dearly loves every man. He longs to see His river flow through the hearts of every person who calls on the name of Jesus Christ.

This will not happen if Christians confuse doctrinal belief with genuine experience. There is a vast difference between doctrinal belief and genuine experience. Just because you have been raised in a Pentecostal or Charismatic tradition does not mean you have experienced the presence and power of God.

Many have heard about it and believe in it but have never experienced it.

Many good Christians have the misdirected belief that doing things decently and in order means rigidly regulating worship and banning manifestations of spirituality or emotions. This misplaced zeal has produced powerless and lifeless churches where the supernatural gifts of the Spirit described in the Epistles are missing entirely. A Church without power cannot reap and keep the harvest of souls in this last generation. God is not pleased with extra-biblical doctrines that promote *"a form of godliness, but denying the power thereof."*[8] Jesus said we would have *power* when the Holy Ghost comes upon us.

I am sure the arrival of the Holy Spirit in the Upper Room didn't precisely match our modem definitions of decently and in order, but it was God. In my case, I wasn't prepared to accept the freedom that revival would bring to Brownsville Assembly of God Church, so God dealt with me until I changed. He touched me so powerfully that I lay helpless in front of my congregation the entire length of service after service. This occurred for over a month after the revival began! When God finally let me stand before the congregation again, I had my pointer finger back in my pocket where it belonged.

Obstacle #7: Self-Condemnation: You must remember who you are. The lies of the enemy cannot condemn the sons of God.

Satan is called *"the accuser of the brethren"*[9] for a good reason. Just when we think we have left every distraction behind and shut the door to our prayer closets, a familiar accusing voice begins to rehearse our faults and failures in agonizing detail. We need to remember this wise advice—consider the source. Any time you separate yourself from your daily routine for a time of focused prayer in God's presence, your accuser is waiting. He will do anything to keep you from praying, and condemnation is one of his favorite tactics. The surprising fact is that if Satan should ever take a holiday, we would more than likely continue his condemning work without his help! This may be why John the apostle said:

> *And hereby we know that we are of the truth, and shall assure our hearts before him. For if our heart condemn us, God is greater than our heart, and knoweth all things. Beloved, if our heart condemn us not, then have we confidence toward God. And whatsoever we ask, we receive of him, because we keep his commandments, and do those things that are pleasing in his sight* (1 John 3:19-22).

When you come before God in prayer, you should first *assure* yourself of your standing in Him. Remind yourself that Jesus Christ alone has qualified you to enter the presence of God. Ask Holy Spirit to reveal any unconfessed sin that might be blocking your communication with God—then confess it and repent. Begin to praise God and quote Scriptures that declare your identity in Christ. Rejoice in God's Word and declare:

> *I am the righteousness of God in Christ. I am a new creature, created in God's image for His good*

pleasure. I am a child of God and an heir of all His promises through Christ Jesus. Greater is He that is in me than he that is in the world! There is no condemnation against me because I am in Christ Jesus, and I walk after the Spirit and not after the flesh.[10]

Obstacle #8: Disrespect to a Spouse: Suppressing the anointing and gifts in your spouse will rob you of the full power needed to break through a heaven of brass.

Likewise, ye husbands, dwell with [your wives] *according to knowledge, giving honour unto the wife, as unto the weaker vessel, and as being heirs together of the grace of life; that your prayers be not hindered* (1 Peter 3:7).

Many marriages are destroyed and prayer is hindered when familiarity in marital relationships spawns contempt. Although contempt born from familiarity is commonplace, this tendency need not destroy our homes. Love and genuine concern expressed by each member of a well-kept marriage do much to keep this destroyer away.

However, when marriage partners begin to take each other for granted, forgetting the small gestures that show love and appreciation, a gradual contempt may start to grow silently day by day. It is particularly easy for men to treat their wives with rudeness and outright disrespect since they often have the dominant personality in the home.

This is not God's plan. Man is a woman's protector, not her destroyer. Everything he does should build her up, not tear her down. This should be true of his attitudes, words, and actions as he shows gentle consideration for her needs and personal wishes. Praise will earn him respect much sooner than selfish domination. Careful listening and thoughtful kindnesses will turn her heart toward him.

Too often, marriages are torn apart by judgments and assumptions that breed contempt. Beware lest Satan, using his most compelling lie against you, implants in your mind the thought that your spouse does not recognize or appreciate your anointing and the destiny God has placed on your life. This lie tears at the fabric of your spiritual strength and the very beliefs that identify you as a believer. Once the enemy has convinced you that your spouse does not share deeply in your life and work, you begin to follow a dangerous path that separates you from your spouse—even while you live under the same roof! These separate life paths will most certainly result in tragic pain and may even lead to separation and divorce.

The heavens are brass over those willing to accept such demonic lies. Every other temptation waits for its turn to humiliate and destroy the one who separates from their spouse because of ministry and calling. Strength is drained, and the safety and protection of the family unit are compromised. Temptation, sickness, depression, discouragement, rebellion, and even disobedience among your children may all result from this breach.

Now an ominous sense of loneliness and abandonment creeps into the heart of family members, and there is no longer a sense of destiny and hope. Trust is gone, and the helpmate principle no longer functions. Inevitably, the bond of love and safety that once ruled the household fades into nothing more than a memory.

Of course, I understand that in very few and rare cases, the separated spouse does not want to accept the call of God on the other spouse's life. Do not assume that this is true for you. In most marriages where separation occurs because of ministry and calling, one spouse has simply believed the lie that his partner does not have what it takes to walk where the "anointed spouse" must walk. Although this problem is prevalent and can be found on both sides of a marriage, it is most often the woman who is the target of this vicious attack.

Safeguard your marriage by recognizing that differences in perspective and calling do not necessarily mean that your spouse does not support you. Be careful not to let assumptions about your spouse's commitment to you, your ministry, or Christ rob you of the blessings and joys committed marriage partners can find. Two are always stronger than one. Value and safeguard that strength, being attentive to the needs and giftings of each marriage partner. Above all, pray together. Couples who pray together discover much about themselves, their marriage, and their ministries that they would not otherwise learn. Then trust God to safeguard your hearts and minds. In so doing, you will keep the skies over your home clear and open.

Hunger and Prayer

Hunger for "more of God" is at the heart of genuinely effective prayer. It seems that the more you seek God, the more you desire Him. Yet this hunger of the heart will also draw the most depraved man and the most hardened backslider to the altar of God. Take heart if your life is entangled with one or more of the obstacles discussed here. Your hunger for more has brought you this far, and it will take you the rest of the way to wholeness if you yield to each gentle tug on your heart by the Holy Spirit.

As a result of the Brownsville Revival, both ministers and laypeople worldwide were attracted to prayer in a fresh way. Churches from across the nations of the earth endeavored to make their churches into houses of prayer. Revival makes you realize that without prayer, there will be no power, deliverance, or a spirit of liberty in the house of God. People regularly come and speak with me privately as I travel across America. They share how revival moved them into the arena of powerful intercessory prayer and the difference it has made in their ministries and churches.

God doesn't look at our titles and ministerial credentials. He is not impressed by them. He looks at our hearts!

Endnotes

1. See Matthew 21:13.
2. See 1 Samuel 2:12–4:22.
3. James Strong, *The Comprehensive Concordance to the Bible* (Iowa Falls, IA: World Bible Publishers, n.d.), regard (Heb., #7200).
4. Ibid.
5. See 1 Corinthians 12:11.
6. John 8:7b.
7. Revelation 12:10.

8. 2 Timothy 3:5.

9. Revelation 12:10.

10. See 2 Corinthians 5:21,17; Genesis 1:26; Revelation 4:11; Romans 8:16-17; 1 John 4:4; Romans 8:1.

CHAPTER 4

CLEANSE THE WATERS SO THE RIVER WILL FLOW

I believe that an uncontrolled sex drive is the greatest hindrance to an individual's prayer life. For three weekends in a row during the revival, a striking blonde woman came to service with a couple I had never seen. Even though the Spirit of God visibly touched the three during the services, they didn't come forward to receive Christ. I wanted to meet them, but they left so quickly after the services that I couldn't reach them. They vanished after the third Sunday.

Several months later, on the exact day I had finished a 13-day fast, my executive assistant, Rose Compton, knocked on my office door and said, "Pastor, we have an emergency out here. Do you have a few moments to see this lady?" I knew by the look on Rose's face that something was seriously wrong, so I told her to bring the lady in.

When the woman entered my office, I was appalled by the look of death I saw on her. Her face was ashen-gray, her blonde hair was unkempt and in disarray, her sunken eyes were dull and red-rimmed. It was clear she was being tormented. I knew I had never met her before, but there was something familiar about her appearance. Then I remembered—this was the blonde woman who had come to the Sunday services months before. Now, I barely recognized her.

After Rose introduced the visitor, I said, "I think I remember you from some of our Sunday services. Didn't you attend some services with a redheaded woman and her husband?"

"Yes, Pastor, that was me. I just wish I had never left."

"What happened to you? Are you okay?" The young woman's eyes filled with tears.

She told me that several weeks after she stopped coming to revival, she was driving along a deserted stretch of highway one rainy night, and she saw a young woman walking beside the road. She felt sorry for the woman, so she stopped and offered her a ride. She ended up taking the hitchhiker home, where she fed her, got her some dry clothes, and tried to comfort her.

The young woman in my office looked down for a moment and then said, "I don't know how it happened. I had never had any thoughts or desires in that direction, but somehow she seduced me, and we ended up in bed together in a lesbian relationship." This woman had been a virgin up until that time, but the hitchhiker managed to manipulate her well-meaning desire to comfort and help. She looked up at me in her shame and said, "I'll never forget what she said when it was over. As she left the room, she looked back at me and said, 'Oh, by the way, I'm a witch.' Something sinister immediately crept over me."

From that night forward, the woman's life quickly fell apart. By allowing herself to be seduced into having lesbian relations with the witch, she had opened her life to demonic oppression. Evil spirits began to come right through her bedroom wall in the middle of the night. The near-constant torment made her unable to sleep. She lost her appetite and began to lose any ability or desire to take care of herself.

The enemy realized this young woman was almost ready to receive Christ after visiting the church, so he ordered a principality, an evil architect, to hatch a plan and lay a trap. He connived to make the heavens over her head brass. As a result, this woman nearly lost her soul and possibly her life.

In the end, she came to the church because it was the one place she knew she could find help. She wanted to be free, so I led her in a prayer of repentance, and she received Jesus Christ as her Lord. Then the battle began. The power of the Holy Ghost flowed through me like a river that day because of the fast I had just completed. The Holy Spirit used me to cast some powerful demons out of the woman, after which she renounced all ties to the dark world. It was the grace of *God* that Satan hadn't snuffed out her life before she found deliverance through Jesus Christ. She almost waited too long.

Satan has spent thousands of years perfecting his traps, snares, and enticements. The Bible says we are not ignorant of his devices.[1] Still, most Christians act like they *are immune to the wiles of the evil one* when they are not. Fewer believers would underestimate or dismiss Satan's devices if they knew the secret to his success: He uses *our desires and lusts* as bait to lure us into his snares in the same way a deer hunter uses musk, scents, or salt licks to attract bucks to a deer stand.

One Obstacle Confronts Us All

I believe one of the greatest hindrances to an individual's prayer life is an uncontrolled sex drive. I am not talking about some isolated problem affecting only a few people. I believe more than 80 percent of all Christians above the age of 12 struggle every day with some aspect of their sexual desires. (The remaining 20 percent may not experience as many challenges because they have had a significant drop in their sexual drive due to advanced age or physical problems.)

Heavens of brass are the inevitable consequence when we yield to temptations and unlawfully exploit the sexual desires that God meant for good. Our response to these desires hinders our prayers, and it also helps Satan thicken the skies over our heads. Thus, our struggles with sexual desires can affect our walk with God, as well as our marriages, finances, and churches. I am convinced that very few people understand the consequences of violating God's Word concerning sexual activity. God said:

> *Therefore shall a man leave his father and his mother, and shall cleave unto his wife: and they shall be one flesh* (Genesis 2:24).

The Hebrew word for *cleave* is *dabaq;* it means "to be joined together as in sexual intercourse."[2] Paul repeated this Old Testament passage in Greek in his letter to the Ephesians. The English translation reads:

> *For this cause shall a man leave his father and mother, and shall be joined unto his wife, and they two shall be one flesh* (Ephesians 5:31).

The Greek word for *joined* is *proskollao,* which means "to be adhered to," referring to deep intimacy. The first part of the word, *pros,* means "forward to, toward," and *kollao* means "to glue."[3] God made man and woman to *proskollao,* to blend in sexual union face to face so their spirits and bodies will blend in spiritual and physical intimacy. This produces an ecstatic blending of body and spirit within the marriage bond that involves our entire beings.

In contrast, the Greek word describing the mating of animals is *kollao.* This refers to a sexual act that is not performed face to face. It is nothing more than physical mating. During mating season, dogs, horses, and other animals move casually from one sex partner to another. Although some species tend to have one mate for life, they procreate through *kollao,* a sexual act that has no spiritual effect.

A man receives much more from his mate than a physical release. He gets a deep sense of nurturing, spiritual replenishment, and refreshment in union with her. A woman receives a profound sense of security as she draws from her husband's love. She is nurtured through caring intimacy with her husband and protector. Sex is part of God's plan and is intensely personal and pleasurable. However, when uncontrolled individuals *kollao* like animals, they violate God's plan and suffer severe consequences.

What? know ye not that he which is joined to an harlot is one body? for two, saith he, shall be one flesh. But he that is joined unto the Lord is one spirit. Flee fornication. Every sin that a man doeth is without the body; but he that committeth fornication sinneth against his own body (1 Corinthians 6:16-18).

Sex Is Like a Camera

Sex works just like the eye of a camera. When the shutter release button is pushed, the eye inside snaps open, and whatever enters through the camera lens is exposed on the film. If that camera has been aimed and deliberately focused, it can produce a beautiful picture of a rose, sunset, snow-covered mountain, or beautiful glacier. Cameras were made to be centered on an object or person and focused precisely, so they could produce beautiful pictures to be enjoyed for a lifetime.

On the other hand, what happens if you haphazardly swing the camera and fire off shot after shot? What happens if you accidentally shoot a picture as you put it into your pocket? The camera shutter will automatically click. Whatever is captured on the lens at that moment—such as a blurry shot of the carpet—will be permanently exposed on the film inside. If a camera is used indiscriminately, whatever the camera lens is exposed to will be developed on the film.

In human intercourse, the "lens" of the spirits of a man and woman opens automatically and is exposed to everything within the other person. The Bible says we become "one" with whomever we join.[4] If a man or a woman unites with a prostitute, they become "one" with the prostitute, along with every other partner the prostitute has ever had!

It is a fact that a sexually promiscuous person can pass along sexually transmitted diseases they received from any previous partner. Millions of people have discovered this too late in the age of deadly sexually transmitted diseases, like the AIDS virus. Similarly, when the witch seduced the blonde woman, the "shutter" of her spirit automatically opened, and she was exposed to the demonic forces at work in that witch. Until the blood of Jesus cleansed her, the heavens over her head turned to brass, and her life became hell on earth.

How Is Sex Supposed to Work?

God intends for a man and woman to be engaged or betrothed for a while. The word *betrothed* means that you have promised and reserved yourself for marriage to another person of the opposite sex. This should be a period of time when you study your intended mate and find out what kind of background they have.

If you are a man, you should ask yourself, "How has my fiancée been raised? Is she good wife material? Does she have the potential of a homemaker? Does she know how to cook? Is she too closely connected to her family to move away should the need arise? Will she run to Daddy every time a decision needs to be made?" Assess her character and see if there is spiritual pollution in her family.

If you are a woman, ask yourself, "Is there witchcraft, fortune-telling, or astrology in his family background? Does alcoholism, drug abuse, or physical abuse run in the family? What was he taught about God? What does he think about child-rearing and discipline in the home? Will he make a good father and priest over our home?"

You may ask, "Isn't love all we need? Why is this so important?" This is important because when you join sexually on your wedding night, the lens of your spirit will open, and you will be bonded to whatever is within your spouse. At the same time, whatever is within your spirit will flow back into your marriage partner. Every person your spouse has been with, everything they believe, and all the darkness surrounding them will be linked with and bonded to *you!* Intercourse is not just a physical act. The entirety of who you are is transferred during sexual union. This is why God ordained that one woman joins with one man for life. This is also why repentance and deliverance are so essential before marriage.

The blood of Jesus cleanses you from sin and washes your spirit from the pollution of your past. If you know this sinful history is in your life or your future spouse's life, it is much better to repent and receive deliverance before marriage. You need fresh film in your camera, so let the Holy Spirit put all negative things under the blood.

Many couples are married for years before they discover that their past is affecting their marriage relationship. It is never too late to repent of old skeletons that still rattle in your closet. It is never too late for the Holy Spirit to release you from those old demonic influences. The sooner they are dealt with, the sooner the Lord Jesus can begin the healing process and restore your marriage to the satisfying covenant God intended it to be.

The fulfillment found in the marriage bed is essential for your well-being. Since you lose part of yourself when you give yourself in sex to someone, God arranged for you to find what you lost in the countenance or face of your spouse. One reason you are to join together face to face is that God made human beings with a "countenance." The human face has the unique ability to display the glory of God. Only humans were made with this capacity—not a donkey, rhino, zebra, or elephant. No other animal was created with this extraordinary potential to display the glory of God. When Moses came down from the mountain, he had to veil his face because of the glory of God on his countenance![5]

We are like reflectors or mirrors in a marriage relationship. Our faces reflect our spirits. This is expressed through our countenance, whether we are sad, glad, worried, or pleased. When we lose ourselves in sexual union, it is reflected as love, satisfaction, and confidence. When there is no one there for us to love, be committed to, and reflect, we are lonely and feel the deficiency. If a relationship is not in the bonds of matrimony, we can't receive what we need. It is blocked by sin.

If you walk into the average American classroom filled with teenagers in the seventh through the twelfth grade, you will notice that many of them are apathetic. They have skipped the discipline of eating a balanced meal and have gratified themselves with desserts and junk foods. Now they are terminally bored. Their attire is sloppy, they've lost their zest for life, and some of them are even suicidal. Why? They became sexually active at a young age. They've been involved in the *kollao* mating process—they've mated like animals solely for a physical thrill and hormonal release—with no thought of cleaving for life. They've known only the temporary relationship inspired by lust, not the covenant relationship motivated by a lifelong commitment to somebody in the marriage bed. They've given themselves away to virtual strangers, and each time they lose something with no hope of receiving back what they lost through the countenance of a spouse in holy wedlock. They are dying of loneliness, and they know something is missing, but they don't know what. Therefore, those in the ministry must not shy away from boldly telling the truth regarding illicit sexual activities.

Each time these young people engage in *kollao,* they lose a bit more of their self-esteem and pride. Although they feel unfulfilled and insecure, they usually will not face the truth of their loss. "Hey, I'm sexually active," they say. "I ought to be happy. They call me the stud of the school, but why am I so unhappy? Why have I been drinking so much lately?" These teens are trying to drown their troubles with alcohol and mood-altering drugs because they are reaping the repercussions of choosing to abandon God's way of living.

It is the same story with the "glitterati" and the so-called "beautiful people" in the entertainment capitals of Hollywood, Nashville, and New York City. They have fame, talent, popularity, money, and the sexual favors of almost anybody they desire. Why do they snort cocaine and drink so much that they end their careers in jail or in the arms of a prostitute? It is because you can't defy God's Word without paying the price. Remember, God has life fixed so it won't work without Christ. Sin always comes with built-in consequences. When a person has unrepented sin, the heavens will begin to brass over them. Sin must be repented of to open the heavens. If you regard iniquity, the Lord will not hear you.

If I regard iniquity in my heart, the Lord will not hear me (Psalm 66:18).

God's Plan Takes More Than Anatomy

The animal sex act isn't unique; it is just a matter of having anatomical interaction. The animal kingdom is a reminder that it doesn't take brains, commitment, or a single good character attribute—the things needed to be good parents and lifelong mates. God has a better plan, and it is exciting and rewarding. He commands us to leave and cleave for life.[6]

My precious wife, Brenda, has always made me feel secure in her love. She makes me feel like I am the best thing that ever happened to her. In reality, she is the best thing that ever happened to me. I am not interested in *anyone* else, and she doesn't desire anyone else but me. There is security, joy, fulfillment, and happiness in our relationship. We were both virgins when we married many years ago, and our marriage relationship has been one of joy and fulfillment because we've done things God's way.

If I were to yield to temptation and have an affair, several things would happen. First, I would be hit with guilt that would paralyze every aspect of my life. Second, I would be violating everything that matters the most to me: my relationship with God, my body, my marriage vows, Brenda, and my children. Third, I would begin to suffer. My finances would suffer along with other relationships. My health would surely suffer since the Bible says that a dart would shoot through my liver![7] The Hebrew word for *liver* is *kabed*, or "heavy," and the liver is the heaviest of the internal organs.[8] It comes from the root word *kabod*, the word for "glory." Could it be God is saying that if we join with a harlot or adulterer, a dart will be shot through our glory?

If you are facing the temptation to have sex outside of marriage, ask yourself this question: "Is it really worth it?" I know you want to say, "Oh, but when you're tempted and sexually excited, it's difficult to say you're not interested." My friend, your body may say, "Go for it," but neither your body nor the devil will tell you the truth. Sexual sin brings shame and reproach that will stay with you for the rest of your days. Remember, hormones have no conscience!

Avoid Sexual Entanglement

A young man stood before our congregation in a revival service and told the following story. He testified that God called him to be an evangelist, but when he went away to Bible school, his friends began to ridicule him. He ended up dropping out of Bible school, after which he got entangled in pornography and sexual sin. So far had he fallen that he gave up his dream of preaching the Gospel. Thank God he was drawn to the revival, where he repented of his sin. The sad thing is that he didn't have to fall into sin in the first place. If I've heard that kind of testimony one time, I've heard it a thousand times; and for everyone restored to the Kingdom, countless others never escaped Satan's snare.

Modern America has become a beehive of illicit sexual escapades. You may be a blood-washed believer, but once you walk out of the confines of your godly home, you are susceptible to temptation that could lead to sin. Don't be ignorant of Satan's devices. You may say, "Oh Brother Kilpatrick, you are preaching to the wrong person." No, I'm preaching to the right person because nobody is exempt!

I remember the time a preacher at a conference said, "Bless God, there is one thing I'll never do. I'll never be unfaithful to my bride." Before the next conference, he had fallen into sexual sin. Beware of haughty declarations you cannot fulfill. Walk humbly before God. Live cautiously and lean on the Lord with all of your being. Paul said:

> *For I say, through the grace given unto me, to every man that is among you, not to think of himself more highly than he ought to think* (Romans 12:3).

We are saved and preserved by grace, not by willpower or performance. This is especially important for men because of the strong sex drive God has given them.

The Waters of Human Sexuality in the Bible

The Bible speaks of our human sexuality in terms of "waters." The Book of Proverbs refers to a cistern, a well, and a fountain:

> *Drink waters out of thine own cistern, and running waters out of thine own well. Let thy fountains be dispersed abroad, and rivers of waters in the streets. Let them be only thine own, and not strangers' with thee. Let thy fountain be blessed: and rejoice with the wife of thy youth* (Proverbs 5:15-18).

1. The Virgin: A Cistern of Untapped Water

The Bible depicts a virgin as a "cistern," an untapped well. Her pure waters are sealed until the day of her marriage. When she marries a man who has committed his life to her, she allows him to uncover her well and drink of her waters. Once a virgin marries and becomes sexually active with her husband, she is considered a "well."

2. *The Married Woman: A Well of Refreshing Water for Her Husband*

A married woman, like a well, is a cistern continually filled with deep, still, refreshing water. She takes pleasure in intimacy. She enjoys this the most about her relationship with her husband—the intimacy, sweetness, and kindness he shows her. Thus, when the Scriptures refer to *drinking waters out of thine own cistern and running waters out of thine own well*, they tell you to have sex only with your own mate after marriage.

3. *The Married Man: A Fountain*

A man has a strong sex drive, much like a fountain has a stream of water driven by an internal force. He satisfies this strong drive when he is sexually active with his wife.

When both partners in a marriage flow together within the relationship as God designed it, their sexual union brings both the man and woman *satisfaction* and *ecstasy*. Both are refreshed, renewed, strengthened, and reassured in their love for one another. If, however, the marriage bed is forsaken for whatever reason, both are put at risk.

The man is at the most significant risk because of his sexual drive. He needs sexual relations with his wife regularly. On the other hand, the woman is at risk when her spouse withholds the intimacy and gentle care she needs. This is why the apostle Paul warned Christian couples:

Nevertheless, to avoid fornication, let every man have his own wife, and let every woman have her own husband. Let the husband render unto the wife due benevolence: and likewise also the wife unto the husband. The wife hath not power of her own body, but the husband: and likewise also the husband hath not power of his own body, but the wife. Defraud ye not one the other [don't withhold sexual relations], *except it be with consent for a time, that ye may give yourselves to fasting and prayer; and come together again, that Satan tempt you not for your incontinency* (1 Corinthians 7:2-5).

Stolen Waters: Sex Outside Marriage

Long before there was knowledge about venereal diseases, or the spiritual laws of transference, the Bible perfectly described the symptoms of sexual sin. Proverbs 23:27 says:

For a whore is a deep ditch; and a strange woman is a narrow pit.

A "deep ditch" and a "narrow pit" are not exactly sweet metaphors for purity and refreshment in sexual activity. The water in a ditch is diseased, and the water in a narrow pit is contaminated and polluted with all kinds of insects and diseases brooding and breeding there.

The Book of Proverbs also likens sex with a prostitute to "stolen waters."

A foolish woman is clamorous: she is simple, and knoweth nothing. ...she saith to him, Stolen waters

are sweet, and bread eaten in secret is pleasant.
But he knoweth not that the dead are there; and
that her guests are in the depths of hell (Proverbs
9:13,16-18).

In other words, sex with a prostitute or an adulteress is like partaking of impure, polluted, and disease-filled water, which brings sickness and death.

God said that a pure woman is a well, but a whore is a deep ditch, and an adulteress is a narrow pit. God planned for women to be pure cisterns and refreshing wells. He ordained every man to be a pure fountain, dedicated totally to one cistern and well for life. He created the reproductive organs of humanity and set specific laws into motion to govern our relationships. If we deviate from what He has ordained, we reap automatic, built-in consequences. God doesn't have to lean over His throne and say, "I caught you." Just like He put the laws of gravity into effect on the earth, He set the laws that govern human sexuality. If you try to defy gravity by jumping from a high place, you will be seriously injured or killed. In the same way, if you defy God's plan for sexual behavior, you will have the devil to pay.

You may say, "What I do sexually is my business and nobody else's!" Don't believe it! The Bible says:

For the ways of man are before the eyes of the Lord,
and he pondereth all his goings (Proverbs 5:21).

Pensacola is a Navy town, and while we pastored there, we worked with military personnel for many years. When sailors finally stepped from the deck of their ship in Italy or Hawaii after an unbroken tour of several months at sea, their hormones were raging. Once on land, many of them would look for a place of sexual release, thinking their time with a prostitute or a paramour was "just a sex act." It was not! When these sailors came home, they soon discovered they were different. Although they didn't understand why, they were anxious, lonely, and depressed. They wondered why they were no longer happy with their spouse and children.

The sailors' problems were that they bonded sexually and spiritually with prostitutes, strangers in distant lands. Not only were they now bonded to these prostitutes, but these individuals were also bonded to the countless other sex partners that these strangers had. My friend, it messes you up when you are unfaithful sexually.

If you are a Christian, you know God traces sin right to your heart and most private thoughts. He knows when you deviate from your spiritual walk and are tempted toward seduction. Temptation is not a sin, but if you ponder and fantasize about committing fornication or being unfaithful to your spouse, you're guilty. Jesus said:

> *Whosoever looketh on a woman to lust after her hath committed adultery with her already in his heart* (Matthew 5:28).

This does not mean that since you've thought of the sin, you should go through with it. Both the thought and the action are wrong. However, when you have sex outside of marriage, not only have you sinned against God, but you have also sinned against yourself. You have tasted stolen waters, thereby violating your wife, family, and your own body. Stop every temptation at the thought stage. If you harbor and savor the temptation in your imagination long enough, it becomes a stronghold.

The apostle Paul gave us the best advice: *"Flee...youthful lusts."*[9] This means you should run away or escape from lustful thoughts or situations. Evangelist Steve Hill said many times, "If you are driving and see a body jogging toward you, don't look to see if it's male or female. If you want your anointing and the power of God to leave like a bird flying off a perch, just start fantasizing and be led away by your lust." I guarantee that the glory and anointing you have sought for so long will leave you in a split second if you grieve the Holy Spirit by clinging to a lustful sin. Sexual pleasure is not worth it!

We need to know that people get involved in sexual sins for several reasons. First, they are curious. Many affairs begin with the illicit thought, "I wonder what it would be like to be with someone else?" Second, they become bored and restless, "My marriage is boring. My spouse doesn't look like they once did." If that's the only reason you got married, your relationship won't last long. God never intended for you to choose a spouse predicated on how they look! Beauty is skin deep, and skin changes with every passing year. What if your wife has a mastectomy or your husband loses an arm in an accident? Will these things suddenly make your marriage vows null and void?

The Temptations Provoked by a Loose Woman

The Bible devotes many verses to warn about the dangerous ways of evil women; therefore, a man must go out of his way to avoid the temptations of loose women. A loose woman is a prostitute, an adulteress, or one who commits fornication. She will not make good "wife material." Not every girl you date is going to make a good wife. She may be a bombshell in the looks department, but that doesn't mean she would make a good wife or mother. She may be built precisely like your fantasy wants her to be built, but what about her character? She could lead you straight to hell. Cities like New Orleans and other pleasure cities have fallen under a tremendous demonic influence because of the seductive wiles of loose women and the unbridled sexual desires of men. The Book of Proverbs says:

And, behold, there met him a woman with the attire of an harlot, and subtil of heart. (She is loud and stubborn; her feet abide not in her house: now is she without, now in the streets, and lieth in wait at every corner.) So she caught him, and kissed him, and with an impudent face said unto him, I have peace offerings with me; this day have I payed my vows. Therefore came I forth to meet thee, diligently to seek thy face, and I have found thee. I have decked my bed with coverings of tapestry, with carved works, with fine linen of Egypt. I have perfumed my bed with myrrh, aloes, and cinnamon. Come, let us take our fill of love until the morning: let us solace ourselves with loves. For the goodman is not at home, he is gone a long journey: he hath taken a bag of money with him, and will come home at the day appointed. With her much fair speech she caused him to yield, with the flattering of her lips she forced him (Proverbs 7:10-21).

This Scripture passage shows a loose woman's various snares to trap a man.

1. A loose woman catches a man's eyes by dressing seductively, carefully exposing parts of her body with low-cut blouses, short skirts, or tight leggings. She walks and moves in overtly sexual ways.

2. A loose woman shocks a man by talking about intimacy without inhibition. Verse 13 of Proverbs chapter 7 describes a bold woman who caught a man and kissed him passionately with lips burning hot with lust. She shocked him by talking about taboo subjects, such as his ability to make love. Her seductive words set his hormones on fire.

3. A loose woman reassures a man, saying, "God put us together." Many a man of God has fallen into sexual sin right in the church building after agreeing to counsel women alone in his office because these women said, "God told me to come to you right away. You are the only one who can help me with my problem, and I just can't wait any longer." The woman in Proverbs 7 bragged that she had just paid her debt for sin under the old covenant law. She had just been to the church of her day.

4. A loose woman tempts a man with stories about how sexy she looks in bed. She describes in vivid detail just what it would be like to have sex with her.

5. A loose woman uses words of flattery and invitation to secure what she wants once she has painted a picture of desire and inflamed a man's sexual desire:

Come, let us take our fill of love until the morning (Proverbs 7:18a).

With her much fair speech she caused him to yield, with the flattering of her lips she forced him (Proverbs 7:21).

A man in love with his Savior and secure in his identity as God's son will not be susceptible to any kind of flattery, least of all the flattery of an ill-intentioned person.

6. A loose woman finally tells a man, "We won't get caught."

An evil woman views sex as a game of power. She is driven to hunt for susceptible men of power and prestige and bend them to her will. She is particularly attracted to men of great visibility, such as preachers, politicians, and well-known businessmen. She is not so much driven by sexual passion but by a desire for illicit power over men. Such a woman will plot and strategize ways to seduce the man in her sights. She might say, "I bet he'll be mine if I build him up and flatter him just right. He doesn't look like he's happy at home." Anyone can become the target of a loose woman—a boss, manager, evangelist, pastor, or politician. If a man falls into her trap, she destroys his very soul. Look at Proverbs 6:32:

But whoso committeth adultery with a woman lack-eth understanding: he that doeth it destroyeth his own soul.

While I have directed much of these recent comments toward men being tempted by provocative, loose women, I want to clarify that being tempted to commit adultery is as common among women as it is for men. Seduction is a compelling strategy of the enemy. Both men and women must be vigilant.

Anyone who commits adultery can destroy their mind, emotions, body, and reputation. They will never again be considered an honorable person once their indiscretion is revealed—and it will be. If Satan doesn't reveal it with the hope of destroying them, God will so He can save them. Adultery is a unique crime because it turns a pure relationship into a polluted one. There is more hope for a thief than for an adulterer because a thief can pay back sevenfold what he has stolen.[10] An adulterer, whether it be a man or a woman, can never pay back what they have stolen.

He goeth after her straightway, as an ox goeth to the slaughter, or as a fool to the correction of the stocks; Till a dart strike through his liver; as a bird hasteth to the snare, and knoweth not that it is for his life (Proverbs 7:22-23).

Obedience Releases the River of God

Isn't it interesting that Jesus performed His first miracle at a wedding and that it had to do with water? If you recall the story in John 2:1-10, Jesus and His disciples were invited to a marriage feast in Cana of Galilee. When the guests called for wine when there was no more, Mary told Jesus the problem. He told the servants of the house to fill large waterpots with water, then dip some out and take it to the master of the feast.

When those worried servants approached those large containers, they couldn't see the miracle in the water. It was only when they obeyed and dipped a ladle into the water that it was turned into wine. People don't understand the miracle God put in the marriage relationship. It only looks like boring, ordinary water to people who view marriage outside God's plan. The Lord knows the miracle power that lies hidden in marriage.

When we dip into the waters of marriage God's way, we discover we are drinking the wine of God! When we honor the *well* of the woman and the *fountain* of the man in obedience to God's plan, He releases a third source of "water" into that marriage relationship—the *river* of His Spirit. The Holy Spirit is also symbolized in Scripture as wine. This completes the miraculous picture of the union of the waters of human sexuality and supernatural spirituality in marriage.

Apply this understanding to the woman at the well in John 4:11-42. It was no coincidence that Jesus met this Samaritan woman beside the well of Jacob. He told her, "Call your husband and come here," implying, "Where is your fountain?" When she said she had no husband, Jesus answered:

> *Thou hast well said, I have no husband: for thou hast had five husbands; and he whom thou now hast is not thy husband: in that saidst thou truly* (John 4:17b-18).

The good news is that Jesus was telling her, "I have water for you that will take away all your sin and shame." He brought this fallen woman hope and confidence.

Most of us know that the blood of Jesus cleanses us from all sin and unrighteousness, but consider what Jesus was saying to this sexually polluted woman who wanted to worship God from a pure heart. He told her about a well of water springing up into everlasting life. This implies an artesian well, a well that yields an inexhaustible supply of fresh water from underneath the surface with great force. Jesus was talking about the river of God, the Holy Spirit. Compare this with His words in the Gospel of John:

> *He that believeth on me, as the scripture hath said, out of his belly shall flow rivers of living water. (But this spake he of the Spirit, which they that believe on him should receive)* (John 7:38-39).

God gave us the blood of His only begotten Son to cleanse us from sin in His sight. He also gave us the river of the Holy Ghost to give us power over sin and Satan in *this* life! Jesus told the disciples, *"But ye shall receive power, after that the Holy Ghost is come upon you"* (Acts 1:8a).

You need more than cleansing from the sin you have already committed. You need the power to overcome the sin you will be tempted to commit today and tomorrow. You need the overwhelming, overcoming, overflowing current of the river of God to flood your banks and refresh your waters that have become polluted through sin.

Bathsheba was the mother of Solomon. She became the wife of David, but only after she committed adultery with David while she was married to another man. When David took her to his bed, Bathsheba became a contaminated well. Thus, when Bathsheba announced that she was pregnant, David plotted to hide his sin by bringing her husband home from the war front. When this man refused to sleep with his wife for reasons of honorable duty as a soldier, David plotted his murder.

After Bathsheba's husband died because of David's cold-blooded plot, she married David and bore a son. When the child died, David was heartbroken that he had broken God's law and was separated from God by sin.

David repented of his sin and turned from it. God, in His mercy, gave David another child. That child would eventually become a wise, rich, and notorious king. Despite David's sin, as well as Solomon's sin with his heathen wives, God, in His great mercy, allowed the genealogy of Jesus Christ to come through that bloodline. These things are beyond our understanding.

Solomon's fall into sin is directly traceable to the tainted spiritual heritage he received from his adulterous parents and to his appetite for forbidden sexual union with hundreds of ungodly women:

> *And he had seven hundred wives, princesses, and three hundred concubines: and his wives turned away his heart. For it came to pass, when Solomon was old, that his wives turned away his heart after other gods: and his heart was not perfect with the*

Lord his God, as was the heart of David his father
(1 Kings 11:3-4).

King Solomon's heart was turned away from God by the 700 wives and 300 concubines he collected to satisfy his lusts, many of them from foreign nations that worshiped demons. What a polluted house!

Again, the best advice for those who want to keep clear heavens overhead is to *"flee...youthful lusts."*[11] The Bible also gives us timeless advice for handling tempting thoughts and fantasies:

> *Casting down imaginations, and every high thing
> that exalteth itself against the knowledge of God,
> and bringing into captivity every thought to the
> obedience of Christ* (2 Corinthians 10:5).

If you have already failed and desire to worship God in purity again, God's Word declares, "Whom the Son sets free is free indeed."[12] Start fresh today and restore the joy of unblocked and unhindered prayer and communion with God!

Endnotes

1. See 2 Corinthians 2:11.
2. Strong's, *dabaq* (Heb., #1692).
3. Strong's, *join* and associated root words (Gr. #4347, #4314, and #2853).
4. See Genesis 2:24; 1 Corinthians 6:16.
5. See Exodus 34:29-33.
6. See Genesis 2:24.
7. See Proverbs 7:23.

8. Strong's, *kabed* (Heb., #3516).

9. 2 Timothy 2:22a.

10. See Proverbs 6:31.

11. 2 Timothy 2:22a.

12. See John 8:36.

CHAPTER 5

GOD'S PRESCRIPTION FOR A BREAKTHROUGH

*Howbeit this kind goeth not
out but by prayer and fasting.*
—MATTHEW 17:21

Through the years, I've seen such a lack of fruit in Christianity that I have seriously wondered, "Lord, how many will make it? Will everyone who is in the Body of Christ be part of the Bride of Christ?" I am concerned about people who call themselves "Christians" yet live a lifestyle that does not match God's Word or the Lord's example. The things they do in their personal lives, and even in their ministries, reflect poorly on everyone who names the name of Jesus. During prayer one day, the Lord said to me, "Not everyone who is in My Body will be in My Bride." That was when I realized that "the Body" has an earthly connotation, but "the Bride" has a heavenly connotation.

God Requires Obedience Above All Other Things

After years of study and holding my peace about this, I want to give you several Scriptures, including some quotes from Jesus, which support my statement. Obedience is all-important. That is why there will be many professors but few possessors.

To Obey Is to Do God's Will

> Not every one that saith unto me, Lord, Lord, shall enter into the kingdom of heaven; but he that doeth the will of my Father which is in heaven. Many will say to me in that day, Lord, Lord, have we not prophesied in thy name? and in thy name have cast out devils? and in thy name done many wonderful works? And then will I profess unto them, I never knew you: depart from me, ye that work iniquity (Matthew 7:21-23).

Jesus said, "Many will say to me in that day [not a few, but many], Lord, Lord, have we not prophesied in thy name?" Jesus wasn't talking about "lost" people. These people knew God. They were professing Christians and acknowledged Jesus as Lord. The Bible says that "no man can say that Jesus is Lord but by the Holy Ghost."[1] They were the real deal, but the Lord said He did not know them (approve of them).

Jesus didn't say they *tried* to cast out devils. He said they cast out devils in His name. These people had the power to cast them out![2] When Jesus sent out the 70 disciples, they also had the power to cast out devils—including Judas Iscariot! You need to remember that it isn't what you do *for* God or how many people you help. The real issue is whether you are in submission to Him.

If you look closely, you will see that Jesus didn't dispute the things the people were saying. He never denied their claims that they prophesied in His name—because they did! He didn't correct them by saying they had given a "false" prophecy. He didn't deny that they had done "many wonderful works" in His name. The problem was that they had not done "the will of the Father." This earned them one of the strongest rebukes in the Bible. Jesus said, *"And then will I profess unto them, I never knew you: depart from me, ye that work iniquity"* (Matt. 7:23).

In effect, Jesus was saying, "I never approved of you, you workers of lawlessness [iniquity] who would have no law over you. You took the gift but left the Giver. You took the anointing but never bowed your knee to the Lord. You are like a wild maverick going off and doing your own thing."

In Matthew 7:23, Jesus didn't simply say, *"I never knew you."* He was quoting a rabbinic phrase everyone understood. Leading scholars of the Greek New Testament, who have studied the Jewish traditions from the Talmud and the Midrash, say that "the words *'I never knew you'* were used by rabbis as a *banish formula.*"[3] This phrase had the authority of a judge's final sentence declared over a disobedient defendant. Jesus is serious about obedience.

It is safe to say that everyone who reads this book can name certain unharnessed mavericks who are out there roaming the Kingdom, doing all kinds of things for God. The problem is that when the Lord says, "Heel!" they turn a deaf ear and keep going headstrong in their so-called ministry. Powerful works and ministries have never been the issue. When the 70 disciples came back to Jesus and said excitedly, "Even the devils are subject to us!" Jesus said:

> *I beheld Satan as lightning fall from heaven.*
> *...rejoice not, that the spirits are subject unto you;*
> *but rather rejoice, because your names are written*
> *in heaven* (Luke 10:18,20).

In other words, Jesus was saying, "I'm not impressed that devils are subject to you. I want to see you obey My commands so you can be part of My Kingdom."

To Obey Is to Prepare for the Coming of Christ

In Matthew 25, Jesus showed us that He demands preparation and foresight from those who wish to attend His wedding banquet. In the parable of the wise and foolish virgins, *all* ten women who were waiting for the bridegroom were virgins. They were *all* asleep, they *all* had lamps, *and* they *all* awoke at the same time. The difference between the five wise virgins and the five foolish virgins became apparent when a cry was made at midnight saying, *"Behold, the bridegroom cometh."*[4] The Bible says that *all ten virgins* woke up and began to trim the wicks on their lamps. Then the five foolish virgins realized all the oil in their lamps had burned, and they had brought no extra oil to refill their lamps.

The five wise virgins were prepared because they had purchased extra oil. However, they refused to share their supply with the five foolish virgins and told them: "Go get your oil at the same place we got ours!"[5] So the foolish virgins went to buy oil. The bridegroom came while they were gone, and they were shut out of the wedding feast.

This is a sobering picture of the last days. You may have a lamp, you may be a virgin, and when the Bridegroom comes, you may awaken with all the other virgins in the Body of Christ. However, if you do not prepare in advance as the Master commanded, you may not be part of His wedding feast. God wants more than suitable clothing, a good education, or the right gifts and religious words. He demands obedience.

Parents want their children to obey. Hugs, kisses, and gifts can't take the place of obedience. Where there is obedience, the expressions of love flow naturally. The same is true of our relationship with God. God fixed life so that it doesn't work without Him! Obedience is the secret weapon of every Christian.

To Obey Is to Seek God Honestly and to Love as He Loves

Sometimes our love for God wanes, and our relationship with Him grows cold from a lack of obedience. Revival revives that which is nearly dead or forgotten. It returns us to our first love, fieriest passion, and deepest conviction. It revitalizes our spirit-man, restoring its rule over the soul and the flesh, and reorders our priorities according to God's will. Revival reaches through a small hole in the heavens of brass and clears the skies for an even mightier outpouring of God's presence.

A flood of dishonesty and hypocrisy has stolen the vigor of the Church. Many of God's people have become masqueraders who stage a parade of pretense every Sunday morning! They say, "We are Christ's disciples," but they ignore His commands. This causes a significant problem because God demands obedience. The Bible provides deep instruction regarding obedience versus disobedience. We need a revival of honesty and holiness in our homes and churches.

Part of the problem is that we seek the gifts of the Spirit instead of the Giver of the gifts. We confess God's Word but don't bother to seek or obey the God of the Word. We preach volumes on love but crucify anyone who dares to disagree with us. We talk holy on Sunday but not on Monday. We argue and leave churches over the slightest differences in doctrine, forgetting that true disciples are to be known not by their doctrine but by their love for one another. We love the excitement and power of revival but are not willing to pay the price of persistently seeking the God of revival. God is not pleased with our façade.

> *Yet they seek me daily, and delight to know my ways...they take delight in approaching to God. Wherefore have we fasted, say they, and thou seest not? wherefore have we afflicted our soul, and thou takest no knowledge? Behold, in the day of your fast ye find pleasure, and exact all your labours. Behold, ye fast for strife and debate, and to smite with the fist of wickedness: ye shall not fast as ye do this day, to make your voice to be heard on high. Is it such a fast that I have chosen? a day for a man to afflict his soul? is it to bow down his head as a bulrush, and*

to spread sackcloth and ashes under him? wilt thou
call this a fast, and an acceptable day to the Lord?
(Isaiah 58:2-5)

God spoke this message to His people through the prophet Isaiah. He was chastising the descendants of Abraham because they had fallen in love with the letter of the law while neglecting the Spirit behind it. In the New Testament, Jesus directed most of His anger toward the religious people, not the sinners!

> God abhors what we think He scarcely notices, and He scarcely notices what we think He abhors.

One evening, a prostitute came to revival wearing red hotpants and a halter top with a bare midriff. When the Holy Spirit touched her heart, she ran down to the altar, repented of her sin, received forgiveness, and was gloriously saved that night. As she kneeled at the altar, I directed three ladies to discreetly form a shield with prayer cloths between her and the congregation. I knew that certain people in the congregation would be distracted or offended by the woman's appearance.

Do you think God was distracted or offended by that young woman's clothing? *Absolutely not!* He was overjoyed to see a lost soul yielding to conviction and unashamedly repenting. He wasn't the least bit embarrassed, and we shouldn't be either. Too many of us have forgotten that the Church is supposed to be a hospital for sinners, not a museum for saints.

God is not impressed by outward appearances but goes out of His way to chastise hypocrisy and dishonesty! These two elements are often primary ingredients in creating a heaven of brass. Jesus confronted the most respected religious leaders of His day with this scathing accusation:

> *Woe unto you, scribes and Pharisees, hypocrites! for ye are like unto whited sepulchres, which indeed appear beautiful outward, but are within full of dead men's bones, and of all uncleanness. Even so ye also outwardly appear righteous unto men, but within ye are full of hypocrisy and iniquity* (Matthew 23:27-28).

To Obey Is to Pray and to Keep God's Chosen Fast

All our problems cannot be attributed to the devil or demon spirits; *disobedience* plays a dominant role. There is probably less genuine prayer going up to Heaven now than ever. If prayer is rare, then true heartfelt, biblical, Spirit-led fasting is rarely practiced in the modern Church! Too many of us take delight in approaching God, hoping to get something from Him. Then we grumble and complain if we don't get it. We even try to manipulate God with guilt and innuendo, just like we manipulate one another. Likewise, when we do fast, we usually do it so that God will hear our prayers better. God doesn't have a hearing problem—we do!

God gave us certain crowbars to help us pry and jar our flesh from the seat of authority so that our spirits can take control. Jesus knew His disciples would face many things as they carried the Gospel into the world. Therefore, He constantly put them in situations where they had to face the risk of failure and stretch their faith. The disciples cast out demons many times, but one day, they encountered a demon so powerful that it refused to obey their commands. Matthew chapter 17 describes this event when the disciples learned about two of the most powerful crowbars God gives us:

> *Then came the disciples to Jesus apart, and said, Why could not we cast him out? And Jesus said unto them, Because of your unbelief: for verily I say unto you, If ye have faith as a grain of mustard seed, ye shall say unto this mountain, Remove hence to yonder place; and it shall remove; and nothing shall be impossible unto you. Howbeit this kind goeth not out but by prayer and fasting* (Matthew 17:19-21).

Some bondages, yokes, bands, and even spirits will release their victims only when someone dares to fast and pray. Business as usual won't do it. God's chosen prescription is fasting and prayer until the powers of evil are defeated.

Spirit-led prayer and fasting turn our eyes from ourselves toward those things on the heart of God. In Isaiah's day, the Jewish religious leaders perfected the art of the fast as a religious exercise. Although they prayed faithfully to God every day, it was only an act because they fasted and prayed with wrong motives. Their eyes were on themselves and the things that pleased men. Therefore, their prayer and fasting yielded no fruit to demonstrate a real encounter with God. The Lord was so disturbed by their behavior that He demanded men observe a different kind of fast.

> *Is not this the fast that I have chosen? to loose the bands of wickedness, to undo the heavy burdens, and to let the oppressed go free, and that ye break every yoke? Is it not to deal thy bread to the hungry, and that thou bring the poor that are cast out to thy house? when thou seest the naked, that thou cover him; and that thou hide not thyself from thine own flesh?* (Isaiah 58:6-7)

The Fast (Life) That Pleases God

These verses list seven key characteristics describing the type of fast (and type of life) that pleases God. They are God's prescription for breaking through the brassiest heavens. He calls us to:

1. Loose the bands of wickedness and undo the heavy burdens.
2. Let the oppressed go free.
3. Break every yoke.
4. Deal thy bread to the hungry.
5. Bring the poor that are cast out into thy house.
6. Cover the naked.
7. Do not hide thyself from thine own flesh.

Each one of these points demands that we add works to our faith. It isn't enough to have faith without action. If our faith is genuine, we must show practical fruit in our actions toward others. If the fruit is missing, we must ask ourselves if our faith is genuine. Thus, if the Church is isolated and out of touch with the needs of people, it is probably because you and I are isolated and out of touch—our faith is not having an impact.

Jesus Christ calls His Church into the world with the good news of the Gospel. God's requirement for us is to pray, fast, and forsake our private religion. We have good news, and we must share it with those who need it!

1. Loose the bands of wickedness and undo the heavy burdens.

According to *Merriam-Webster's Collegiate Dictionary*, a *band* is "something that confines or constricts while allowing a degree of movement; something that binds or restrains legally, morally, or spiritually." The word also means "a group of persons, animals, or things."[6]

Heavy burdens and bands of wickedness may refer to the unlawful restraint and control imposed on vulnerable people by the ungodly systems of this world. These systems may be inspired and guided by Satan's hand, but the truth remains that man's hand is the instrument inflicting pain and hardship on innocent people. God called us to loose these bands and undo the heavy burdens He never intended us to carry. Some of the worst bands and burdens are rooted in religious hypocrisy.

Jesus referred to these heavy burdens when He taught His disciples:

> *All therefore whatsoever they bid you observe, that observe and do; but do not ye after their works: for*

*they say, and do not. For they bind heavy burdens
and grievous to be borne, and lay them on men's
shoulders; but they themselves will not move them
with one of their fingers* (Matthew 23:3-4).

One of the most common bands of wickedness is the false
religious idea that we must be cleaned up and holy before
coming to God. Self-righteous Christians have fostered this lie
for centuries, a lie that has kept countless millions out of God's
Kingdom. This band of wickedness must be destroyed by the
truth that God calls individuals to repent and receive forgiveness. Jesus said it best:

*They that are whole have no need of the physician,
but they that are sick: I came not to call the righteous, but sinners to repentance* (Mark 2:17).

Bands in the Church

Some churches have a degree of freedom that allows them to
advance to a certain point in praise or prayer, but they can't go
any further. In some cases, a band of disobedience or man-made
religious tradition is restraining them. God wants us to release
our preconceived ideas about how He works so He can take us
further in His glory. If we leap into the river of His Spirit with
our whole hearts, we won't live the rest of our days in mourning
because of a void in our spiritual lives.

Even more common are bands that haunt and bind us to
darkness. These bands attached themselves long before we
came to Christ. They keep us from moving ahead in our walk
with Jesus because they prevent us from believing anything will

ever change. This is where the support and encouragement of God's people can make a difference. The Word tells us to bear one another's burdens,[7] rejoice with those who rejoice, and weep with those who weep.[8] This is the purpose of the Body of Christ.

The enemy brings bands of affliction against individuals and families he has targeted for destruction. When we see someone under attack, we shouldn't hesitate to provide support. For example, if someone is battling with a recurring sin or temptation, we can encourage them to redirect their thoughts to things God has done for them. We can also suggest listening to worship music or reading a book to strengthen their faith. We should be ready to stand with them if they fall, even if it is again and again. Believers facing these kinds of problems need special support until they can renew their minds in the Word of God. This care will help them overcome the circumstances that may be causing them to stumble. Even the most stubborn bands that inhibit the growth of believers can be broken, including alcohol, drugs, pornography, eating disorders, homosexuality, and others.

Bands in the World

John, the apostle, said that the whole world lies "in wickedness."[9] Jesus said:

> *Ye are the light of the world. A city that is set on an hill cannot be hid* (Matthew 5:14).
>
> *Ye are the salt of the earth: but if the salt have lost his savour, wherewith shall it be salted? it is thenceforth good for nothing, but to be cast out, and to be trodden under foot of men* (Matthew 5:13).

God does not intend for His people to remain neutral or invisible. He sends us into the world with authority to invade, disturb, and occupy everything Satan has stolen. But our salt isn't salty, our light isn't bright, and the city of God has been hidden through political correctness and compromise. We have blended into the world with such ungodly ease that God's transforming power is too often weakened or completely absent. Revival changes this!

Jesus constantly put His followers on the front line of ministry. He is doing the same thing today. He wants to send us into cities and towns with the Gospel, just like He sent out the 70 in Luke 10:1. His last words before ascending to the Father were words of commission, delegation, and assignment:

> Go ye therefore, and teach all nations, baptizing them in the name of the Father, and of the Son, and of the Holy Ghost: teaching them to observe all things whatsoever I have commanded you: and, lo, I am with you always, even unto the end of the world. Amen (Matthew 28:19-20).

He described those who enter His new covenant in dynamic terms that can only be understood as supernatural:

> And these signs shall follow them that believe; In my name shall they cast out devils; they shall speak with new tongues; they shall take up serpents; and if they drink any deadly thing, it shall not hurt them; they shall lay hands on the sick, and they shall recover (Mark 16:17-18).

These individuals know how to loose bands of wickedness and undo heavy burdens. They are actively doing God's work in the world. Unfortunately, the modern Church often groups these passages with other Bible verses under the teaching, "They passed away with the apostles."

The apostles functioned in the kind of power these passages describe. Throughout the New Testament, we see they aggressively assaulted the kingdom of darkness everywhere they went. They removed the heavy burdens of pharisaic legalism from Jewish believers and untied the weight of darkness that clung to Gentile converts. Others who shared the work of the Gospel also served in this power. Stephen was a deacon, a table waiter, who worked great miracles among the sick. John Mark, a young disciple who outlived Paul and perhaps all the rest of the apostles, also ministered with authority.

Throughout church history, men and women have received power from the Lord to bring deliverance and freedom. The Church can no longer ignore the command to loose the bands of wickedness and undo heavy burdens. To do so would forsake the very lifework of the Church. We cannot accomplish this work apart from the *power* of the Holy Ghost, but accomplish it we must!

2. Let the oppressed go free.

The Bible says:

> *God anointed Jesus of Nazareth with the Holy Ghost and with power: who went about doing good, and healing all that were oppressed of the devil; for God was with him* (Acts 10:38).

The Greek word for *oppression* is *katadunasteuo,* which means "to exercise dominion against."[10] The Hebrew word used in Isaiah 58:6 for *oppressed* is *ratsats,* which means "to crack in pieces, break, bruise, crush, discourage, oppress, or struggle together."[11]

Our world is being oppressed and bruised by a cruel task-master. The Church should be the one bright hope that promises freedom. After all, we represent the living Christ! But where is the evidence that we are releasing the oppressed from the many afflictions that enslave them? Freedom for the down-trodden will not become a reality until the Church begins to emancipate these people in the name of Jesus Christ! Freedom will not come through a new president, psychologist's couch, or a new batch of governmental programs. The only way a tyrant's authority can be removed is for a more powerful ruler to force him from his throne. The oppressed will see the enemy's dominion cast down only when the Church rises in the authority of Jesus Christ, the King of kings and Lord of lords.

Most of the prayers we offer are for ourselves. This must not continue. The whole point of Isaiah 58 is to compel God's people to turn their eyes and desires away from themselves and focus on the needs of oppressed and hurting people. God wants us to get alone with Him and pray and fast for the lost. If we will, He will give us the faith and power to break every band and loose those who are bound.

3. Break every yoke.

A yoke was a sign of absolute slavery and captivity in the ancient world. Yokes were reserved for heavy work animals such as oxen and donkeys. They were also used as vindictive instruments to humiliate defeated prisoners further. When the Philistines wanted to humiliate their most hated enemy, they put a yoke on Samson and made him grind grain, doing the work of an ox.

Yokes also represented a future of captivity and soul-searing subjection. They chafed the necks and rubbed sores on their victims. Often a person who was bound by a yoke was unable to reach their head to relieve an itch, remove something from their eye, or feed themselves. The yoke rendered them helpless. Since yokes were permanently attached, the only way to free a person from a yoke of bondage was to break it into pieces.

This world has functioned under thickened skies for so long that millions of people live in perpetual darkness under a yoke of demonic bondage. Although the Church has been given the keys to hell, death, and the grave, we have failed to exercise this power effectively. What a shame if we fail to rouse ourselves from sleep and snap yokes in Jesus' name! God will hold us responsible for every act of love, kindness, and redemption we choose *not* to do because we love comfort and ease.

4. Deal thy bread to the hungry.

The Jews of Isaiah's day were overly concerned with formulating merely spiritual interpretations of the Scriptures. It seemed that the longer and more religiously they fasted, the more unjustly they treated the people who were outside their religious inner circle. They disdained the poor and considered poverty proof of a man's wickedness and sin, an attitude erroneously held by many Christians today.

The Church has grown accustomed to letting soup kitchens and relief agencies feed the hungry. Once a year, we send double-digit checks to organizations to feed the poor. We might even drop a can or two in the local food bank. In essence, our attitudes say, "We've done our good deed. Now, what's for dinner, Pastor? Preach to us!"

I think we need to reread the Book. The Bible says of the fast God has chosen:

> *Is it not to deal thy* [your] *bread to the hungry?*
> (Isaiah 58:7a)

God wants our charity and sharing to be personal and up close. He wants us to look into the eyes of the hungry and share from our abundance—or even from our need.

There is something about hands-on ministry and sharing that transforms the heart and soul. There is also something about rubbing shoulders with the hungry, lost, and wounded that helps keep our eyes on Jesus Christ and our egos on the ground where they belong. God planned it that way. He knows that when we share our bread with others, we also share love, encouragement, and reassurance that the person we serve is valuable and precious in the sight of God. This is valuable and rare indeed. Our religion becomes a lifestyle of Christlike sharing, loving, and redeeming. After all, if Jesus were to walk among us today, where would we find Him—with the satisfied or the hungry?

This may not sound like a revival message, but it is. The quickest way to doom a revival or a move of God is to keep it within the four walls of a church building. Many of us are fervently praying that we will see revival move beyond the four walls of our churches and spread into our cities and the nations of the earth. True revival invades every area of life, especially those parts where there is pain.

5. Bring the poor that are cast out into thy house.

Perhaps you didn't notice it, but Isaiah used that irritating word "thy [your]" again. Many Christians struggle with the implications of this word. They fall into the error of asking questions such as, "God, what am I supposed to do?" The answer is simple: Follow the leading of the Holy Spirit. The Scriptures say:

> *The steps of a good man are ordered by the Lord: and he delighteth in his way* (Psalm 37:23).

We know this to be true, but we don't act like it.

A church in revival is a growing church that touches thousands of lives. This includes families dealing with the loss of income due to layoffs, sickness, desertion, or untimely death. Often, they struggle through each week trying to carry the financial load. A church that seriously cares for the poor and hungry will learn to recognize and respond to these needs. Like Jesus, they will reach out to meet the spiritual and the physical needs that sharing food and housing can help satisfy. They will learn to trust God to help them fulfill the needs of hurting people as He brings them into their midst.

The wisdom of God is needed any time you consider bringing a stranger into your home. However, the dividends of sharing our bounty and shelter with others are immeasurable. Families who make it a practice to open their homes to those facing real crises consistently demonstrate a more profound joy and vibrancy in their walk with God. They witness the miraculous on a day-to-day basis as they share with their guests until God takes them from a deep need to total supply. Empty religion has no chance when the miraculous provision of God and the genuine love of Christ are on the scene.

6. Cover the naked.

When Scripture says, *"when **thou** seest the naked, that thou cover him,"*[12] God wants to remove this job from formal institutions and put it into our hands. Our response to cover someone's nakedness should be instant, with no time to premeditate!

The naked can be many people, including those exposed to the elements and those damaged by accusers' words. Anytime you see someone in need, be quick to act on their behalf.

Also, be quick to cover believers who have fallen into sin and repented. The Bible says:

> Hatred stirreth up strifes: but love covereth all sins (Proverbs 10:12).

We are too quick to call for a lynch party when someone in our churches sins. If there is genuine repentance, we need to quickly hide their nakedness with love and encouragement. God never said that we wouldn't fail in this life. He did say:

> For a just man falleth seven times, and riseth up again (Proverbs 24:16a).

7. *Do not hide thyself from thine own flesh.*

Have you ever heard someone say, "Well, you can pick your friends, but you're stuck with family"? This homespun proverb explains why people are guilty of hiding from members of their families. It also explains why many people refuse to commit and submit to a local family of believers. We don't have the option to pick and choose our relatives—neither is God asking for our opinion.

Too many Christians have accepted the wander and roam plan of the world, casting off all obligations to family members, as well as commitments to the church. This is quite dangerous since family and church life are paramount in God's plan. The character of God is best formed in the heat and pressure of long-term, mandatory fellowship with individuals who may or may not agree with you on every detail. More character growth and learning occur in the crucible of family life than in any other area of human existence. When you can't escape from someone's company, you are forced to get along with them.

The family is God's safety net. Modern society has tried to dismantle the family. However, the family structure has worked for thousands of years in every culture. There was family long before welfare agencies, government assistance programs, and Social Security. The family provided for the physical necessities of its members and policed those among them who were not diligent about seeking work or meeting their responsibilities. This is virtually impossible for monolithic government agencies. Even the Church has fallen into the "let the government do it" mentality.

Personal responsibility and duty were once at the heart of family relationships. Children knew they had an inherent responsibility to care for their parents in old age, just as their parents had cared for them in infancy. The sick, disabled, and failing were never abandoned but were cared for. After all, they were family. When personal responsibility and duty are discarded, the family safety net fails. It is time for the Church to restore God's standard of commitment to every Christian home and congregation. Paul made this rule of the new covenant clear:

> *But if any provide not for his own, and specially for those of his own house, he hath denied the faith, and is worse than an infidel* (1 Timothy 5:8).

One reason the Jews have prospered in virtually every country and culture they live in is because they take care of family. If a man settles in a new city and establishes a business there, family members generally work in the business and help it to become stable.

Once someone in the family becomes an adult, the business owner is expected to train them in the family business and either offer them a position there or help them establish a new business. Profits tend to be funneled back into family businesses and the local Jewish community. Likewise, if a family member gets in trouble or needs someone to speak for them in a time of need, the family is there. If a father dies, leaving a widow and children, the family supports them financially and later trains the children for placement in productive jobs. Most loans are made within the community, and few ever default on these family loans.

Two are better than one; because they have a good reward for their labour. For if they fall, the one will lift up his fellow: but woe to him that is alone when he falleth; for he hath not another to help him up. Again, if two lie together, then they have heat: but how can one be warm alone? And if one prevail against him, two shall withstand him; and a three-fold cord is not quickly broken (Ecclesiastes 4:9-12).

God established the family and the Church for good reasons. The union of Christ, the family, and the Church form a threefold cord upon which we can safely build our lives and effectively minister to the hurting. Revival produces God's chosen fast and takes the river of God and His practical provisions into every street and byway.

Endnotes

1. 1 Corinthians 12:3.

2. Matthew 12:29.

3. H.L. Strack and P. Billerbeck, *Kommentar zum Neuen Testament ans Talmust end Midrasch*, 6 vols. (Munich: C.H. Beck, 1965) in Fritz Reinecker and Cleon Rogers, *A Linguistic Key to the Greek New Testament* (Grand Rapids, MI: The Zondervan Corporation, 1976, 1980), 21-22.

4. Matthew 25:6.

5. See Matthew 25:9.

6. *Merriam-Webster's Collegiate Dictionary*, 10th ed. (Springfield, MA: Merriam-Webster, Inc., 1994), 89.

7. See Galatians 6:2.

8. See Romans 12:15.

9. 1 John 5:19.

10. Strong's, *oppressed*, (Gr., #2616).

11. Strong's, (Heb., #7533).

12. Isaiah 58:7b.

CHAPTER 6

IS THERE LEPROSY
IN YOUR HOUSE?

God has a dream for your home and wants it to be a haven. His desire is for your family and guests to be content when you sit down for fellowship. He intends for your dwelling place to be a productive, fertile garden where His Spirit reigns and you can speak freely about Him. Your home, as God prescribed it, should be a place filled with a rich atmosphere of love and acceptance. Words of revelation knowledge should frequently fall from your lips as you speak freely about revival and the moving of God's Spirit.

In your holy house, dedicated to God and sealed in peace, the Holy Spirit can speak directly to your heart with anointed words, helping you win souls and free the hurting. The divine Teacher is welcomed as He makes the Word of God come alive in your heart, burning its truth deeply into your spirit. The Comforter can come over you with divine creativity and direction and order your steps for the day ahead even as you sleep. God is pleased to dwell in this type of house and finds great joy in the love and fellowship there.

Does Your Home Match God's Dream?

Not all homes match this picture. If we are honest, few of us would say that God's dream is lived out in our houses. How would you describe your house? Do you barely shut the door of your home following a church service before all hell breaks loose? Are you and your spouse constantly fighting? Are temper tantrums and fits of rage commonplace? Do you regularly fill your children's ears with cutting words, negative comments, and belittling sarcasm? Does bickering over unimportant details fill the rooms of your house? Are verbal battering and emotional abuse so prevalent that your family avoids sharing meals?

If you answered yes to one or more of these questions, something is seriously wrong with your home. You can't ignore the problem by consoling yourself with the knowledge that other people live the same way. Dismissing a problem is never the answer. You must admit you have a problem—a plague is loose in your house, and it is trying to destroy you and your family.

When revival broke out, I noticed people who were touched by the power of God would get up off the floor and go home rejoicing. Sometimes entire families—father, mother, children, grandparents—lay on the floor for hours under the power of God. But on the way home, they ended up in a big fight! Children who had shed tears under the anointing of God became rude, disobedient, and openly challenged their parents and one another.

My heart ached as I heard one story after another from people who were wonderful in church but awful in their homes. I heard this repeatedly from numerous people. I went to the Lord and asked what in the world was going on. Holy Spirit revealed to me that the atmosphere at the church had been purged and cleansed, but they were returning home to an atmosphere that had not been purged and cleansed. Their homes were polluted and contaminated. Therefore, it affected their behavior when they returned home. A person's behavior is greatly influenced by a holy atmosphere as well as an unholy atmosphere.

God Will Not Live with the Devil or His Stuff

As a pastor, I am interested in long-term fruit that can be seen. Genuine revival should bring renewal and refreshing into every area of our lives, no matter where we are. Change evident in the few hours we spend in church each week has little or no value. I began to intercede for these families whose behavior changed so drastically once they entered their home environment. I asked the Lord to show me the root and cure for this prevalent problem. One day, the Lord said to me:

> *If My people don't get rid of the unclean things in their homes and lives, My precious Spirit and glory will not stay very long. I have come to give them the strength to cast out the unclean things.*

The Lord showed me that the holy gifts and anointing these families received from Him in the church services weren't sticking because God's presence was clashing with the climate of their homes. God is reviving us to provide the strength and resolve to rid our homes of unclean things that vex us.

Holiness was a characteristic of the Brownsville Revival because it is a characteristic of God. When He answered our prayers for a visitation of His presence, the poverty of our holiness was evident in every service. Even the most mature and holy among us sensed an urgent need to repent before God and be cleansed anew by Him.

The need for repentance does not stop when we leave the church building. God requires holiness in all aspects of our lives. He comes to touch us, help us, sanctify us, and fix us, but He will not bless our sin. We cannot expect the Lord's presence to stay with us if we go home from church to a house tainted by pornography, R-rated movies, and other willful sins. We would be dismayed should the Lord choose to enter this type of home because the joy we find in God's presence would soon be exchanged for weeping. While the sudden appearance of God to a holy people brings unspeakable joy, the same appearance in an unclean congregation or household brings devastation and destruction. If we choose to forsake the Lord and return to our sinful ways, then the very things God provided that should work for us now work against us. God will not justify our sin.

Those who refuse to take God's overcoming anointing home through lack of obedience spurn the work of God in their lives. They choose to return to the sin for which they repented. How difficult their path will be!

For it had been better for them not to have known the way of righteousness, than, after they have known it, to turn from the holy commandment delivered unto them. But it is happened unto them

according to the true proverb, The dog is turned to
his own vomit again; and the sow that was washed
to her wallowing in the mire (2 Peter 2:21-22).

God is omniscient. He cannot be fooled, and He sees all things. He knows precisely what you are thinking at this moment, and He sees those things you keep hidden because you are ashamed of them. He sees and remembers what happens behind the closed doors of your office and in your home. He hears your phone conversations and sees your text messages. He can describe the title and contents of every movie on your shelf, every video you have watched, and knows the website history you erased. He hears your words and knows the times you misuse His name or speak with disrespect to your spouse, parents, or children.

Sin Makes a House Barren or Sterile

One of the telltale signs of a spiritually troubled home is what I call sterility. This barrenness makes your home an unsuitable place to pray. You may find it difficult or unenjoyable to pray at home. A brooding heaviness permeates the air, and attitudes and moods are often volatile. (This same sterility can affect local congregations. A troubled church will usually have a stifling environment that seems to wither its members and everything connected with it.)

Children do not flourish in a sterile or barren environment. They need the covering and protection of their parents to ward off spiritual assaults. When parents go wrong, vulnerable children suffer. Some children I've ministered to were withered because their fathers were very harsh, raging and cursing at them. Others bore the effects of parental conflict because one parent turned on the other. Still other children sustained spiritual damage because their fathers were constantly cursing and criticizing their wives. The constant stream of negative words hurt not only the women but also the children.

Negative words and deeds are always destructive. Like a hot desert wind scorches and withers all living things, the hot breath of criticism and cutting words withers the lives of those in the home. This produces sterility and eventual death. Since the spirits of children are particularly susceptible to negative words and deeds, they suffer whether the negative, damning words are spoken directly to them or another person.

Each of us must honestly ask ourselves, "Is there fertility or sterility in my home? Are the people under my roof budding, thriving, and appropriately maturing, or has their growth been stunted by withering words and deeds?" Sometimes we have difficulty giving an honest appraisal of our homes. It is time to carefully evaluate and observe how family members respond to us and others. For example, are your spouse and your children afraid of you? Do they tense up when you walk by? Are you unpredictable or strange in your ways, responding one way today and another way tomorrow? Do you have a bad attitude? Do the people who live with you try to figure out whether you are in a good mood or a bad mood so they can alter their behavior accordingly? Some children can't wait to turn 18, so they can leave that sterile, dry, and oppressed place called home.

You have serious problems in your house if happiness, joy, and vitality are absent. The measures of love, joy, peace, and contentment you see in the faces of your children and your spouse are the same measures of freedom the Holy Ghost enjoys in your house!

This honest evaluation of ourselves and our homes can, at times, be quite disconcerting, but don't despair. God's Word offers a cure for the things that plague us. God knows the exact problems abiding in your house, and He has already provided both the diagnosis and the cure.

Help for a Sterile Home

First, let us diagnose the cause of spiritual sterility in our homes. The Book of Leviticus sets forth a detailed procedure.

Tell the Priest: "There Is a Plague in My House!"

> And the Lord spake unto Moses and unto Aaron, saying, When ye be come into the land of Canaan, which I give to you for a possession, and I put the plague of leprosy in a house of the land of your possession; and he that owneth the house shall come and tell the priest, saying, It seemeth to me there is as it were a plague in the house (Leviticus 14:33-35).

Examine the House

> Then the priest shall command that they empty the house, before the priest go into it to see the plague, that all that is in the house be not made unclean: and afterward the priest shall go in to see the house: and he shall look on the plague, and, behold, if the plague be in the walls of the house with hollow

strakes, greenish or reddish, which in sight are lower than the wall; then the priest shall go out of the house to the door of the house, and shut up the house seven days (Leviticus 14:36-38).

Cleanse the House

And the priest shall come again the seventh day, and shall look: and, behold, if the plague be spread in the walls of the house; then the priest shall command that they take away the stones in which the plague is, and they shall cast them into an unclean place without the city: and he shall cause the house to be scraped within round about, and they shall pour out the dust that they scrape off without the city into an unclean place: and they shall take other stones, and put them in the place of those stones; and he shall take other stones, and shall plaister the house (Leviticus 14:39-42).

If the House Is Still Unclean, Don't Ignore the Symptoms

And if the plague come again, and break out in the house, after that he hath taken away the stones, and after he hath scraped the house, and after it is plaistered; then the priest shall come and look, and, behold, if the plague be spread in the house, it is a fretting [angry] leprosy in the house; it is unclean. And he shall break down the house, the stones of it, and the timber thereof, and all the morter of the house; and he shall carry them forth out of the city into an unclean place (Leviticus 14:43-45).

Personal Cleansing and Declaring the Cure

Moreover he that goeth into the house all the while that it is shut up shall be unclean until the even. And he that lieth in the house shall wash his clothes; and he that eateth in the house shall wash his clothes. And if the priest shall come in, and look upon it, and, behold, the plague hath not spread in the house, after the house was plaistered: then the priest shall pronounce the house clean, because the plague is healed (Leviticus 14:46-48).

Atonement for the House

And he shall take to cleanse the house two birds, and cedar wood, and scarlet, and hyssop: and he shall kill the one of the birds in an earthen vessel over running water: and he shall take the cedar wood, and the hyssop, and the scarlet, and the living bird, and dip them in the blood of the slain bird, and in the running water, and sprinkle the house seven times: and he shall cleanse the house with the blood of the bird, and with the running water, and with the living bird, and with the cedar wood, and with the hyssop, and with the scarlet: but he shall let go the living bird out of the city into the open fields, and make an atonement for the house: and it shall be clean. This is the law for all manner of plague of leprosy, and scall (Leviticus 14:49-54).

Leviticus is one of the first five books of the Bible. These five books are called the Pentateuch and were written by Moses. Leviticus deals with the Levitical law that God prescribed for the children of Israel. These spiritual and physical house-cleaning instructions were given to Moses before God's people entered Canaan. While this promised land would be a wonderful home with many blessings, God also established some precautions that His people needed to follow.

1.   Tell the Priest: "There Is a Plague in My House!"

God promised His people an exceedingly good land that flowed with milk and honey. He said He would give them houses they didn't build, wells they didn't dig, and vineyards they didn't plant.[1] However, these blessings came with instructions and a warning.

Specifically, God told His people to examine the walls of their houses, whether they built them or moved into houses others had built. He wanted them to pay close attention to the walls of their dwellings. If they felt there was a scall or leprosy or observed anything unusual in the walls of their homes, they were to go to the priest immediately and tell him, "I think there is a plague in my house!"

The Bible says that God is the one who put the plague of leprosy in these houses. Why would He do that? He used the plague of leprosy as a litmus test to reveal the presence of evil spirits in these Canaanite dwellings.

A chemist or medical lab worker knows the dyes, specimen stains, and chemicals used in medical tests. Many, if not most, of the major tests performed in medical laboratories use dyes, tinctures, and chemical reagents to reveal things hidden from the naked eye. God used the plague of leprosy described in Leviticus chapter 14 in the same manner.

2. Examine the House

Should a man find leprosy in his walls and run to tell the priest, the priest would tell the occupants to remove everything so he could inspect every inch of the house's walls, floors, and foundation. If green or red streaks were found, the priest would close the house and set it under quarantine. After seven days, he was to inspect it again. If the streaks had spread, the priest and homeowners were to follow God's instructions without delay.

3. Cleanse the House

If the plague had spread, the family living in the house had some serious housecleaning to do. This was not the "scrub with cleanser until the stains are gone" kind of cleaning. It required a significant effort, including removing every contaminated stone from the dwelling's walls, floors, and foundation. Not only the contaminants in plain view were to be removed but also those hidden. Even the dust from the mortar chiseled out from between the stones had to be scraped off just in case the mortar contained the plague. When all contaminated stones and mortar, including the dust, had been removed, they were to be carted to an unclean place far from the house or city and dumped there. Only then could the homeowners begin to replace the impure materials with fresh stones and mortar.

Once the renovation was complete, only time would tell if the plague would return.

4. If the House Is Still Unclean, Don't Ignore the Symptoms

In some cases, the priest would return to the house for inspection and find red and green streaks running along the walls again. Even after all the trouble of inspecting the dwelling's walls, floors, and foundation, as well as removing and replacing stones and mortar, evidence of leprosy would still be found. In those cases, the priests were to warn the family not to sleep, eat, or even sit in the house because it would make them unclean. They had to vacate the dwelling because a "fretting" or "angry" leprosy had been found.

Finding the evidence of fretting leprosy in a house revealed the presence of devilish contamination. Remember, God is omnipotent (all-powerful), omnipresent (existing in all places, at all times), and omniscient (seeing and knowing all things). He cannot be surprised or caught off guard by anyone or anything. If fretting leprosy was found in a house, He allowed it there for a reason. That reason is of vital importance for *you* today!

God told Moses about the plague of leprosy long before the Jews reached Canaan because He wanted to make a point: "Moses, if a priest walks into a house and finds this plague of fretting leprosy, be very careful to dismantle the entire house immediately, block by block, timber by timber. Tear it down to the ground since deadly pollution is hidden in that house. My people must be careful to do this, or they will suffer because of the corruption."

The ancient Jewish rabbis taught that God devised this plague because of Israel's delay in entering the Promised Land due to their fear, doubt, and unbelief. Their sin transformed what should have been a 40-day trip across the desert into a 40-year trek of death for that entire generation. By the time the new generation stepped onto the soil of Canaan, the news of Israel's mighty God had already reached the Canaanites. They knew well the stories of Jehovah, the Hebrew God. Not surprisingly, they were fearful, wondering how they would keep these unstoppable invaders from overrunning their land. Throughout those 40 years of fretting and stewing, the Canaanite people told and retold the stories of the drowning of Pharaoh's army in the Red Sea. They looked for ways to protect themselves and defend their property. Finally, they began to say, "If that God is going to bring those Hebrews into our land, if He is going to give them our houses, our wells, our vineyards, and our land of milk and honey, we are going to hide our riches so that they have a hard time finding them."

Thus, according to the rabbis, the Canaanites began to ingeniously hoard their silver and gold. Sometimes they devised elaborate schemes to hide it, hoping that the Jews would eventually leave so they could retrieve their riches. At other times, they chose to convert their precious metals into smaller artifacts so that their treasures were not readily available to the invaders.

As the Israelites' years of desert wandering continued, the Canaanites and Amorites melted down more and more of their silver and gold. They made little demon gods or idols that were easily hidden in the walls and foundations of their homes.

When Israel finally entered the land of Canaan, they moved into homes that were cursed by the presence of demonic idols hidden by the people who preceded them in the land.

God devised the plague of leprosy to warn His people of the existence of these pagan idols. Many times, when the Israelites pulled down the walls and dug up the floors of their homes after the telltale sign of red and green streaks had appeared, they found these small demon gods of gold and silver hidden in secret compartments throughout their dwellings. God knew all along that these idols were there. He used the plague of leprosy to share this information with His people. Why didn't God just ignore the presence of these idols? It's for the same reason He cannot ignore the sin in your house. He will not co-exist with evil.

5. Personal Cleansing and Declaring the Cure

Due to ignorance, many Christian homes become houses of worship for demon gods. God provided the sacrifice of Jesus Christ to atone for our sins. His blood cleanses and protects all who accept Him as Savior, but He will not share our home with demon gods. Many Christians expect Him to do just that. They have given room to other gods without intending to do so and now suffer the effects of this contamination. This often happens when Christians purchase and bring home items with demon gods attached.

Call me a narrow-minded, superstitious preacher if you want, but God's Word clearly states He will not share a dwelling with your household gods.

And the Philistines took the ark of God, and brought it from Ebenezer unto Ashdod. When the

Philistines took the ark of God, they brought it into the house of Dagon, and set it by Dagon. And when they of Ashdod arose early on the morrow, behold, Dagon was fallen upon his face to the earth before the ark of the Lord. And they took Dagon, and set him in his place again. And when they arose early on the morrow morning, behold, Dagon was fallen upon his face to the ground before the ark of the Lord; and the head of Dagon and both the palms of his hands were cut off upon the threshold; only the stump of Dagon was left to him. Therefore neither the priests of Dagon, nor any that come into Dagon's house, tread on the threshold of Dagon in Ashdod unto this day. But the hand of the Lord was heavy upon them of Ashdod, and he destroyed them, and smote them with emerods, even Ashdod and the coasts thereof. And when the men of Ashdod saw that it was so, they said, The ark of the God of Israel shall not abide with us: for his hand is sore upon us, and upon Dagon our god (1 Samuel 5:1-7).

You are flirting with fire when you decorate your home with foreign gods. It is very risky to have anything in your home with evil or occult influences. There are fetishes and images that have demonic origins. These things were created and named for the worship and veneration of evil spirits, not God! Even if you say, "Well, I certainly don't worship them," you still owe God an explanation of why you openly display them, which was the custom of pagans, a practice that still dominates many religions. I'm telling you, God will not tolerate devils or the items of devils. Neither will He continue to grace your home if you refuse to clean out the filth contaminating it.

Many people like to attend church because they enjoy the peace and comfort of God's presence. They say, "This is so wonderful. I feel the presence of God here." God is not content for you to experience His presence only while at church. He wants you to experience His presence in your home. However, I must tell you this gift does not come cheap. We must engage in fervent prayer and do some serious housecleaning before our homes are a suitable place for the Lord to dwell. Remember, God is very particular about the company He keeps. He will not live with sin and evil actions.

You can go into a revival service, fall on the floor, and shake like a leaf in an autumn wind, but I'd say, "So what?" if you go right back home and live the same kind of sinful life that God has warned you about for the past five years. Who is it that you are trying to fool? No matter how much you run, dance, or shake, or how many glowing testimonies you give about the glorious visitation of God you experienced, don't try to tell me that the anointing of God is in your house if you continue to treat your spouse like dirt, continue to view questionable movies, look at pornographic websites, or read books that contain ungodly contents. Likewise, don't play holy in the church house if you still abuse others, including your spouse or children, with temper tantrums, scathing accusations, or ungodly language.

Long before the revival in Pensacola, we had to discipline some members. We would say, "Look, you are free to come to this church, but you are not going to carry a card saying you are a member here while you continue to live in blatant sin. We obeyed the Bible and disciplined people if they were involved in an adulterous affair, living a homosexual lifestyle, or were entangled in other evident unrepented sins. If they still refused to forsake and repent of their willful sin, we refused to even eat a meal with them. If a man wanted a position of leadership or authority in the church, we wanted to know how he ruled his household. Scripture says:

> *For if a man know not how to rule his own house, how shall he take care of the church of God?* (1 Timothy 3:5)

I still believe in holiness because the Bible says that "without holiness, no man will see God."[2] God will not move until we deal with sin, rebellion, sexual promiscuity, and other unholy habits. Such behavior hurts our Christian witness and brings reproach to the name of the Lord. It causes dryness to develop in our worship, prayer, and preaching. God's Spirit becomes so grieved that He will withdraw His presence and allow us to enjoy the sin we preferred over Him. That is when the spiritual atmosphere in our homes and churches becomes dry and stagnant.

Joshua confidently crossed the River Jordan armed with a promise from God, but hidden sin cut short God's provision, protection, and blessing! After the Israelites destroyed the great fortified city of Jericho, Joshua sent a smaller group to wipe out a tiny town called Ai. He was shocked when the outnumbered men of that city humiliated Israel's army! When Joshua started complaining to God about "failed promises," the Lord told him to get off his face and deal with sin in the camp if he expected Jehovah to fight on his behalf. Look what God told Joshua:

> *Therefore the children of Israel could not stand before their enemies, but turned their backs before their enemies, because they were accursed: neither will I be with you any more, except ye destroy the accursed from among you. Up, sanctify the people, and say, Sanctify yourselves against to morrow: for thus saith the Lord God of Israel, There is an accursed thing in the midst of thee, O Israel: thou canst not stand before thine enemies, until ye take away the accursed thing from among you* (Joshua 7:12-13).

God was saying, "I won't be with you anymore except you deal with the sin. Get up and get to it!"

6. Atonement for the House

God was serious about the power these demon gods represented in the spirit realm. Demon gods are lightning rods for demonic activity. Spiritual problems require spiritual solutions.

> *And he shall take to cleanse the house two birds, and cedar wood, and scarlet, and hyssop: and he shall kill the one of the birds...and he shall take the cedar wood, and the hyssop, and the scarlet, and the living bird, and dip them in the blood of the slain bird, and in the running water, and sprinkle the house seven times: and he shall cleanse the house with the*

blood of the bird, and with the running water, and with the living bird, and with the cedar wood, and with the hyssop, and with the scarlet: but he shall let go the living bird out of the city into the open fields, and make an atonement for the house: and it shall be clean (Leviticus 14:49-53).

God demanded more than mere human cleanup efforts where demonic contamination was found; He required *atonement,* which means "to cover over."[3] (It has also been said that atonement means "at-one-ment" with God.) Atonement was always made through the blood of an innocent sacrifice to highlight the horror of man's sin. After the sacrifice of atonement had been made, the priest was to take hyssop (a bitter herb), dip it in the blood of the slain sacrifice, and sprinkle the house seven times. This ceremony of atonement had to be performed to purify the house.

The Law of Moses required a sacrifice of atonement for every contaminated house. In other words, if there was sin, there had to be blood, innocent blood. The house could not be cleansed in the spirit realm until that blood was shed. Whatever contamination the priest found had to be removed and atoned for.

A plaque of leprosy meant something was wrong—both in the physical and spirit realms. If you have appendicitis, you experience fever and pain in your body. If you focus on treating just the fever or pain, you could lose your life! The fever and pain are merely symptoms of a more profound and much more severe problem. There are symptoms in your home that are just as real and dangerous as the physical symptoms of a serious disease. Something is not right—do not keep ignoring the symptoms!

The Holy Ghost wants to warn you if leprosy is in your house. You could be suffering from a sterile environment just as surely as the Israelites suffered when green and red streaks appeared along the walls of their houses. Something in your house must go if you want the anointing and presence of God to stay with you.

Is the Priest on Duty?

If you are a husband or father, I want you to read these words very carefully: *God has called you to be the priest in your home.* If something isn't right, don't bury your head and act like everything is fine. When your wife or children come to you with a concern, listen to them and take an active role in addressing their concerns. By bringing their cares to you, they are instinctively following God's ancient pattern. They are taking their problems to the priest. They want and need you to stand up and be a man.

Get up and examine your house! See if the walls of protection around your family have been breached in any way. Rid your home of the devil if he has taken up residence. Get the snake out of your house! Yes, I do believe that demons can oppress a house. If you don't believe me, just get on one of those pornographic websites, start watching it late at night, and see how quickly some demons move into your home. You need to declare, "I will rise up, stand watch, and take my duties seriously. I'm going to look at the walls and foundations of every room with a magnifying glass. I won't be quiet until I find out if something is present that shouldn't be." You won't have to search long. Holy Spirit will give you discernment that will lead you right to the plague.

Let Holy Spirit guide you. He will impress on your spirit those things which grieve and offend Him. He may point to where you are dabbling in questionable activities or illicit things that you would never have tolerated in the past. He may warn you of habits and activities that have been part of your home for so many years that you have become inoculated to them. Whatever He shows you, you must thoroughly cleanse. If you don't confess every problem area and wash your house thoroughly, you may even backslide—all because you did not deal with the plagues in your house that Holy Spirit revealed to you. Clean your home well so that uncleanness finds no welcome there.

A perpetually unclean house becomes like a leech from the devil. It draws the anointing out of your life, and as the leech gets fatter and fatter, you get weaker and weaker! This is why Paul said we should *"lay aside every weight, and the sin which doth so easily beset us."* God wants to empower you with boldness to accomplish all that needs to be done. He will not give you rest until you attack everything that opens you and your family to the devil's influence.

Your Words Contain Power

Jesus said:

> *The words that I speak unto you, they are spirit, and they are life* (John 6:63b).

Can the same be said of your words? Do you speak words of life or death? Words are powerful forces. They reveal your heart. Jesus said:

> *A good man out of the good treasure of his heart bringeth forth that which is good; and an evil man out of the evil treasure of his heart bringeth forth that which is evil: for of the abundance of the heart his mouth speaketh* (Luke 6:45).

Your words come from your innermost belly and embody the condition of your spirit. Once your words leave your mouth, the "spirit" of what you say fills the air and begins to rumble around in your home. Whether for good or evil, your words take up residence as you speak them. Like bubbles of air, your words burst and begin to affect the atmosphere. Caustic, biting, negative words spew destructive influences into your environment. On the other hand, loving, affirming, kind words enrich your environment, keeping it fluid and free.

These influences (spirits) then move from one person to the next, to the next, to the next, and so on. The Bible speaks about this "transference of spirits":

> *And the Lord came down in a cloud, and spake unto* [Moses], *and took of the spirit that was upon him, and gave it unto the seventy elders: and it came to pass, that, when the spirit rested upon them, they prophesied, and did not cease* (Numbers 11:25).

A negative influence occurred when the spirit of doubt, fear, and unbelief saturated the ten spies who returned from the Promised Land. These spirits were transferred to the entire nation of Israel![5] The result of this negative transference was that all but two of the adult members of the nation were barred from entering the land that God promised them. They were misled and died as desert wanderers because they accepted the negative spirits of the ten spies.

The words you speak in your home are "spirit." The same is true for the words others say there. As surely as the sun rises each morning, they release whatever is in them. What they release is up to you. Your words and the words of those who enter your home will loose either blessings or curses upon your household. You may be accustomed to lots of choices, but God narrows the choice:

> *I call heaven and earth to record this day against you, that I have set before you life and death, blessing and cursing: therefore choose life, that both thou and thy seed may live* (Deuteronomy 30:19).

There are no alternatives. The words we choose to speak release either life or death. That's it. Period. If we are wise, we will carefully guard the words that come from our mouths and the mouths of those who live in our homes. By exercising authority over words spoken in our homes, we will also monitor the words we permit visitors to speak. When friends visit and you find yourself telling your spouse, "I don't know why, but I always feel like I need a bath when they leave," you would do well to examine carefully the words (spirits) they are depositing into your home.

If your friends are critical or doubtful about the things of God, and if they are slandering and gossiping, here is my pastoral counsel for you—do not invite them back into your home. You may say, "Oh, but we have been friends for years." Perhaps it is time to reconsider that friendship because the time you spend in their company allows their negative attitudes, thoughts, and behavior to be transferred to you.

Difficult as it may be, you must be careful to never put people above God's Word and relationships above principle. To do so is the same as calling the local trash dump and arranging for them to fill your home with a fresh load of garbage. The scents from the smelly garbage will soon permeate your entire house. The same is true of your children's friends. Keep a close watch on their friends.

You can choose to live with the stench, but you should also be prepared for the sterility that will overtake your home. Rotting garbage has a way of leaving a lingering odor. Negative words and ungodly companions have a similar effect. When you allow them into your home, you soon find that the toxic environment destroys life instead of renewing it.

You must make a choice. Will you choose an atmosphere that refreshes, preserves, encourages, and renews all who enter your home, or will you occupy a sterile, lifeless house dominated by anger, strife, sorrow, and death? You cannot blame others for your choice since you alone have the authority to censor what transpires in your home.

God has given you every tool needed to establish a home filled with laughter, peace, respect, and love. He has made you a priest and a king through Jesus Christ.[6] Now, you must put all He has given you to good use. You must obey His Word and yield to the leading of His Spirit. When you are tired of living in a sterile house under skies of brass, no effort or sacrifice will be too great to keep you from cleansing the leprosy from your home. Only then will you be ready to annihilate the plague. God will not bless your home when your behavior and words are motivated by jealousy, hatred, envy, bitterness, dissension, disrespect, or lust.

It's time to clean house! God is waiting at the door. As you sweep all the negative talk, idolatrous loyalties, and ungodly habits out the door, He will enter and fill every room with the sweetness of His Spirit and the power of His anointing. That is what your heart has been longing for.

Remember, if we don't clean our houses, God will not abide in our dwellings. It would be a double standard. He will lift His Spirit and write *Ichabod*—the glory has departed—over the door. I don't know about you, but I'm going to do everything in my power to protect the Dove so it won't be grieved or offended in my home or the church I pastor. I don't want the Dove to fly.

Endnotes

1. See Deuteronomy 6:10-11.
2. See Hebrews 12:14.
3. Strong's, *kaphar* (Heb., #3722).
4. Hebrews 12:1a.
5. See Numbers 13:26–14:4.
6. See Revelation 1:6.

CHAPTER 7

OPENING THE HEAVENS OVER YOUR HOME

I heard something long ago that I will pass on to you: *You deserve what you tolerate!* I have never forgotten this, and I hope that you never forget it either. If a splinter is in your finger, and every time you touch something it causes pain, do not complain about it; either remove the splinter yourself or have it removed. If you don't remove it, you deserve every bit of irritation it causes.

This truth is applicable in many areas of life. If you let your children openly defy you, don't complain that your child is out of control. You are receiving the treatment you deserve, and the situation will continue to worsen until you take action to change the child's behavior. Firm discipline with love is the only solution to your problem. (I know that will require you to trust God's Word more than the failed child-rearing theories of man, but your child will not change until you firmly address the problem.)

A family came to my office for counseling. The father was a big fellow, but he started to cry like a baby when he sat down. He said, "Brother Kilpatrick, can you help us? I can't do anything with my son." I looked at this man and his wife, who were very distinguished-looking, and then looked into the foyer at a miserable teenager. The boy was quite a bit smaller than his father. I said, "You are telling me you can't do anything with your son. Before I say anything else, let me ask you a question: Have you ever spanked him?"

That huge man looked down at his big hands and said, "Well, no. Why?" I heard all I needed to hear. I told the man to take his son home. *Don't bring your neglected child to your pastor and expect him to correct the omissions of the father!* The buck stops with you. You are responsible for your child's behavior.

The closed heaven over your head and the fretting plague in your house will never be removed *until you are ready to stop tolerating sin in your life.* When you are ready to end the devil's rampage, God will blast Satan from his position of influence. If you are ready, here are some questions to ask yourself regarding your home:

1. Is there disorder in your home?
2. Are you robbing God?
3. Are you speaking blessings or curses?
4. Is there anything that holds power over you?
5. Is your home under a curse?
6. Is Satan coming into your home through what you listen to and watch?

Depending on your answers to these questions, you may need to take six corresponding steps to purge your home and clear the heavens. Jesus described Satan's intentions when He said:

> *The thief cometh not, but for to steal, and to kill, and to destroy* (John 10:10a).

Satan's goals all require that he first gain access to your house. Notice that Jesus called Satan "a thief."

> *He that entereth not by the door into the sheepfold, but climbeth up some other way, the same is a thief and a robber. But he that entereth in by the door is the shepherd of the sheep* (John 10:1-2).

A thief does not enter your home through the front door like an invited guest. He looks for another way to enter. Satan is a thief, has always been a thief, and will remain a thief. He is looking for an open window, an unguarded passageway, or a breach in a wall through which he can force his way into your home.

Some homes have many access routes for Satan to use. The questions you just used to evaluate the condition of your own home suggest ways he can gain access and violate your family. Let's look at each question to help you realize how much free access he possesses. Pay particular attention to the first question since it is often Satan's primary pathway.

1. Is there a disorder in your home? Reestablish God's order.

God has set a divine order for the home (and the Church). When this order is in place and functioning well, Satan often begins his sinister attack by creating disorder. This is particularly true when the home is well guarded and the man of the house is functioning in his proper role as a priest. Satan may not assault the man's authority directly but will attempt to subvert his authority by attacking another household member.

This mode of operation is demonstrated in the Book of Genesis. Satan did not go to Adam and attempt to lead him astray; he first went to Eve. He circumvented the head of the first family. Once Satan had convinced Eve to disobey God, it was easier to get Adam to sin. He didn't approach Adam directly but sent Eve to him instead. The resulting events show that disorder is usually followed by doubt, denial, deception, disobedience, division, and death.

Disorder Comes First

The Bible clearly states that the man is the head of the home.

Head of the Man

> *But I would have you know, that the head of every man is Christ; and the head of the woman is the man, and the head of Christ is God* (1 Corinthians 11:3).

The husband's position as the head of the home does not make him superior to the woman. Just as God the Father, Jesus Christ the Son, and the Holy Spirit are all one but with distinct functions and characteristics, husbands and wives have different roles and characteristics. Likewise, just as it is inconceivable that we would try to separate the Trinity, we should not try to separate the husband and wife team. A man and his wife are to be one in every way. They simply have different roles and responsibilities. A woman is not inferior to her husband, and her role and position are not of lesser value or importance. They are merely different. Her place under her husband's authority is God's plan for protecting her and their home.

Head of the Woman

> *Submitting yourselves one to another in the fear of God. Wives, submit yourselves unto your own husbands, as unto the Lord. For the husband is the head of the wife, even as Christ is the head of the church: and he is the saviour of the body. Therefore as the church is subject unto Christ, so let the wives be to their own husbands in every thing. Husbands, love your wives, even as Christ also loved the church, and gave himself for it* (Ephesians 5:21-25).

Jesus carefully maintained the right relationship with His head. He did nothing that He did not first see His Father do.[1] This was a priority for Jesus because the power and authority to fulfill His mission were directly linked to God the Father in unity of purpose, mind, and spirit.

A man and a woman united in marriage need the same unity of purpose, mind, and spirit. When this unity is missing, both husband and wife are open to the guiles of Satan. Similarly, Satan gains access to our homes when a husband or wife assumes the opposite partner's role. God created man to conquer and rule. He placed him as the head of the house to protect it. On the other hand, God carefully designed the woman to bear children and nurture the family in tenderness. Disorder results when either the husband or wife abdicates their appointed roles. Each role is precious and vital for the family's well-being. Unfortunately, the tempter knows how prone we are in today's society to rank one role higher than the other, so he uses this weakness for his gain and our loss.

Had Adam and Eve been clear and strong in their roles, Eve would have deferred to her husband, the protector, when the serpent approached her. As the protector, Adam was equipped with the authority and power to deal with the enemy. Instead of permitting the serpent to deceive Eve, he should have taken measures to prevent the ensuing tragedy. He should have moved in his authority and rebuked that serpent. Instead, like many husbands today, Adam did nothing, and sin entered our world. Because of this disorder, Eve was deceived first, then Adam knowingly sinned. Disorder gave way for Satan to take his deceptive plan further because disorder gave way to doubt.

After Disorder Comes Doubt

Once Satan successfully created disorder in the family, he began to plant doubt in Eve's mind. He carefully unfolded his deceptive plan by saying, "Hath God said?" These words clouded Eve's memory as she tried to recall exactly what God had said.

> *Now the serpent was more subtil than any beast of the field which the Lord God had made. And he said unto the woman, Yea, hath God said, Ye shall not eat of every tree of the garden?* (Genesis 3:1)

The adversary uses the same tactic on us. Consider what happens when someone questions the accuracy of how you remember someone else's words. If you are like most people, you wrinkle your brow and critically scan your memory about what you heard. By the person merely asking a question, doubt is planted that you did not hear or recount the original speaker's words correctly. This doubt must be overcome.

Satan knew full well what God said, and so did the woman until Satan asked the question, "Hath God said?" Only then did doubt enter. When God spoke, they had no reason to doubt. God had spoken. That was it! Satan's question, which was once a closed discussion, suddenly became open to interpretation. Satan put a question mark in Eve's mind about God's word by suggesting a possible alternative to what God said.

This is Satan's method. God speaks with authority and puts a period after His word because it is fixed, final, and unchangeable. On the other hand, Satan operates in the realm of question marks. He wants us to regard God's commands differently, so we are not as likely to obey them implicitly. In truth, he wants us to think God's Word shifts and changes depending on circumstances. We would then be more likely not to believe God's commands and promises and give in to our passing whims and desires. For example, the Scriptures clearly state that Satan's eternal damnation and punishment are inevitable because of Christ's victory on the Cross. The enemy, however, is so skillful at deception that he has convinced many that there is no eternal damnation and punishment—for him or them. Don't be deceived! Doubt is always a prelude to denial.

After Doubt Comes Denial

> *And the woman said unto the serpent, We may eat of the fruit of the trees of the garden: but of the fruit of the tree which is in the midst of the garden, God hath said, Ye shall not eat of it, neither shall ye touch it, lest ye die. And the serpent said unto the woman, Ye shall not surely die* (Genesis 3:2-4).

After Satan stuck a knife in, he twisted the knife by openly contradicting God's words: "Ye shall not surely die." He implied that he had inside knowledge about God's motives by denying God's words. In other words, he was saying, "God didn't really say that you would die."

Make no mistake about it—if Satan can keep you doubting long enough, he will eventually lead you into denial. This puts you in a very vulnerable position. Once he places doubt in your mind in one area, he works around the clock to attack other areas of your life—your marriage, your children, friends, church family, coworkers, and boss. Each relationship becomes a target area, and the great deceiver attempts to plant doubt so he can lead you into denial. Should his plan succeed, you could eventually abandon the people and things you hold dear, including your loved ones, your faith in God, and even your salvation through the Lord Jesus Christ.

Do not tolerate the doubt Satan plants in your mind, for doubt leads to denial, which leads to deception. Satan does not have inside information; he just wants you to believe that he does!

After Denial Comes Deception

Deception is the process of rejecting truth in favor of a lie.

> *And the serpent said unto the woman, Ye shall not surely die: for God doth know that in the day ye eat thereof, then your eyes shall be opened, and ye shall be as gods, knowing good and evil. And when the woman saw that the tree was good for food, and that it was pleasant to the eyes, and a tree to be desired to make one wise* (Genesis 3:4-6).

Once the serpent challenged Eve's memory of God's words and caused her to doubt that she had heard correctly, he quickly presumed to speak for God. Satan denied that God meant what He said. He brought into question God's motives and directly contradicted God's words and intentions. With the words *"for God doth know,"* Satan planted in Eve's mind the idea that God was keeping something from her. How subtly the deceiver worked.

Satan's plan worked. With a few short sentences, Eve took the bait. She began to look at the tree of the knowledge of good and evil in a new way. Under the influence of the deceiver, she decided the tree was *"good for food...pleasant to the eyes, and a tree to be desired to make one wise."* It was none of the above.

Once Satan gets you to believe wrong is right and right is wrong, he is well on the way to damning you—and not only you but those in your realm of influence. Our culture is rapidly converting to this upside-down view of life. It is no wonder America is full of deceived, disobedient people.

After Deception Comes Disobedience

> *And when the woman saw...she took of the fruit thereof, and did eat, and gave also unto her husband with her; and he did eat* (Genesis 3:6).

Deception invariably leads to disobedience and partaking of forbidden things. People living in disobedience believe they can make it work out in the end. They think that they can "have their cake and eat it too." Sin and death now become experiential knowledge (Hebrew *yada)* because they believe they can sin like the devil in this life and talk their way into Heaven's gate when the time comes. So thoroughly does Satan pervert their understanding of right and wrong that they develop a distorted perception of God Himself. They say, "If God is a good God, He would never send me to hell." The problem with this is that God is not like man. He does not lie. He says what He means and means what He says. Once He says something, there is no room for discussion, negotiation, or special privileges.

King Saul learned this the hard way. He thought God would bend the rule of righteousness just for him. He soon found out that transgression equals disobedience, no matter how you look at it or try to justify it.

> *Behold, to obey is better than sacrifice, and to hearken than the fat of rams. For rebellion is as the sin of witchcraft, and stubbornness is as iniquity and idolatry. Because thou hast rejected the word of the Lord, he hath also rejected thee* (1 Samuel 15:22-23).

After Disobedience Comes Division

More than half of American marriages end in divorce because the division has crept into the home. Adam and Eve experienced a division that followed disobedience. When God asked Adam to explain what happened, Adam started pointing fingers of blame and division. In a few words, "that woman You gave me," Adam accused both God and Eve of being the reason for his disobedience.

Adam pointed the accusing finger everywhere but where it belonged—toward himself. At that moment, his oneness with his Creator and the helpmate God had given him was lost. Sin had separated Adam and Eve from each other, from God, and, as they would soon learn, from their paradise home. The consequence of sin applied to Adam and Eve and every man and woman since. Their appetite for one bite of forbidden fruit earned the entire human race a sentence of death. God drove them from the garden so they wouldn't eat of the tree of life and be stuck forever in their fallen state.

We are no different from Adam and Eve. Our willful disobedience affects not only us but also every family member.

Parents are the Head of Children

Children, obey your parents in the Lord: for this is right. Honour thy father and mother; which is the first commandment with promise; that it may be well with thee, and thou mayest live long on the earth. And, ye fathers, provoke not your children to wrath: but bring them up in the nurture and admonition of the Lord (Ephesians 6:1-4).

Parents are often physically separated by living in separate households or emotionally detached. They may live in the same house but do what they want without concern for the other marriage partner's needs and wishes. This division is often where our children are caught in Satan's deceptive schemes. At first, they may avoid obedience by pitting one parent against another: "Mom said..." or "Dad lets me...." Over time, this can degenerate so that the child takes one parent's side or emotionally withdraws from both.

Even in relatively healthy households where parents are not separated, they must present a united front to their children. Should they neglect this, the child may be deceived into believing that obedience is optional. Then the entire family is deprived of the love, peace, and joy God originally planned for the well-being of every family. The death of the family unit as God designed it is inevitable when sin and disobedience lead to separation and division. Trust is broken, loyalties are divided, and loving fellowship and support are lost as family members succumb to the delusion of individual autonomy. Obedience becomes a thing of the past.

After Division Comes Death

> *But now being made free from sin, and become servants to God, ye have your fruit unto holiness, and the end everlasting life. For the wages of sin is death; but the gift of God is eternal life through Jesus Christ our Lord* (Romans 6:22-23).

Death reigns where there is disorder, doubt, denial, deception, disobedience, and division. It begins with disorder. Either we see no reason to stay within God's divine order, or the downward spiral toward death has been in motion for so long that we do not realize we are out of order.

Restoring God's order in our homes requires us to work our way back, undoing each step that led to our family's demise. Obedience is often the first thing we must restore. A home where rebellion is tolerated will show evidence of defilement and decay. You might believe the foolish theories of rebellious college professors and fanciful pediatricians, but having order in your home is essential to God. That "expert" or popular magazine may say your disobedient children are just going through a phase. However, the Bible says one of the signs of the coming of the Lord is that children shall revolt against their parents in disobedience and destruction.[2] Many times, we pay attention to anyone except God, and we are paying a hellish price for it.

A look at our public schools and the state of our homes tells the story. Disobedience among our youth is a sign of the times; however, disobedience does not have to be accepted in your home. Your children may exhibit disobedience, but they will only continue this if you continue to tolerate their bad behavior.

I grew up without a father in the house. My mother was just under five feet tall, but when she went outside for a switch to correct the error of my ways, I knew that I was about to suffer the consequences of my disobedience. I had a godly fear of my mother, although I was more than two feet taller than her for many years.

Before I thought about being bad, I always thought about Mama. She used to make me drag my six-foot frame outside to our peach tree to cut off a switch for my correction. When I would return with some anemic, puny excuse for a switch, she would send me back out again, saying, "No boy, you get back out there, and cut a decent switch!" When I came back with a second switch, I would say, "Mama, I got you a good one!" hoping to touch her heart with my newfound zeal. It never quite worked that way because Mama would say, "Bend over, boy!" That was when I knew my sin had found me out, and my fate was sealed.

When Mama was finished with me, I had no trouble discerning right from wrong; and if my memory was poor, my bottom reminded me of the straight and narrow. I loved my mother dearly, but I also respected her with a healthy fear. That mixture of fear and love has profoundly impacted my relationship with God. I have a healthy fear of God today because I developed a healthy fear of my mother in my early years. I tell young people, "If you do not have a healthy respect for your father and mother, you will never respect your schoolteacher or your principal. Neither will you respect a police officer, a judge, the authority in your church, or God Himself. A lack of the fear of God is a sure ticket to hell."

Sometimes parents tell me they love their children and don't want to lose their friendship by correcting them. I tell them, "Listen, God did not call you to be a friend to your children; He called you to be a parent." Parents must tell their children the truth, not just what they want to hear. It never crossed my mind to wonder whether my children liked me or not. All I knew was that I wanted peace in my home. That will never happen if you don't discipline your child in *moderation and love.*

My sons will testify today that I occasionally had to spank them. Before I spanked one of them, I always read the Bible to him, carefully showing him in the Scriptures why I had to administer corporal punishment. Then I would spank him exactly as I had promised. A few minutes after I spanked him, I would take my boy onto my lap and love him. While I loved and hugged him close, I'd say, "Son, I love you so much. That is why I had to correct you." I would then drive off in my car and go to the same secluded spot to cry. That was my pattern: I read the Word, spanked my son, loved him, then cried alone.

Today, my boys are strong, committed Christians. Even as grown men, they love God and respect my authority. Before my oldest son married and moved out of the house, I told him, "Son, I'd appreciate it if you wouldn't work on Sundays. I disapprove of you working on Sundays because God commanded that you should not work on the Sabbath.[3] If you honor the Lord in this way, He will bless you with a good job. Make the right decision now, son."

He said, "Okay, Dad." Sure enough, God provided a great job and has blessed him because he honored his father and the Word of the Lord.

It pays to demand obedience in your home. Disobedience in your home causes the heavens over your head to become brass and separates you from God and His blessings. A pattern of disobedience also separates you from the members of your family. Trust, love, mutual encouragement, and support are lost.

2. Are you robbing God? Rid your house of dishonesty and falsely gained wealth.

Will a man rob God? Yet ye have robbed me. But ye say, Wherein have we robbed thee? In tithes and offerings. Ye are cursed with a curse: for ye have robbed me, even this whole nation (Malachi 3:8-9).

Through the prophet Malachi, God promised He would open the windows of Heaven over those who give Him tithes and offerings. He also warned that the heavens would be closed over those who chose to rob Him by withholding tithes and offerings. I must tell you that this principle goes far beyond tithes and offerings. God warns against every imaginable type of greed and lust for money. Greed and holiness do not mix!

As you assess the condition of your home and take the corrective steps to restore holiness and freedom, you would do well to consider whether you are withholding anything from God or others that rightly belongs to them.

Is there *dishonest* gain in your home? Are you hiding and hoarding gambling money, stolen property, or money from unholy sources? That money has spiritual toxins on it! It was gained the wrong way. Look at these powerful Scriptures:

Wealth gotten by vanity shall be diminished: but he that gathereth by labour shall increase (Proverbs 13:11).

An inheritance may be gotten hastily at the beginning; but the end thereof shall not be blessed (Proverbs 20:21).

Is there *hidden* gain in your house? Are you tucking away money you've hidden from the government to avoid paying your fair share of taxes? Are you clinging to an inheritance by keeping a more significant portion than your rightful share? Such gain brings a curse upon your house. I've seen godly people "go to the devil" when a family inheritance goes to probate court. They come under the power of the devil and bow their knees to the false god of mammon—much to the detriment of their Christian witness! I've personally known many good families who were destroyed by greed over an inheritance.

Perhaps you deliberately deceive your parents, your spouse, or your children so you can amass wealth at their expense. God knows what you are doing and will repay your iniquity. Perhaps your dishonesty extends to God's tithe, and you selfishly keep what belongs to the Lord. Beware! I firmly believe there is coming a time when we will see the restoration of the immediate, visible judgment of God, such as was seen in Acts 5 when Ananias and Sapphira were struck dead for lying to the Holy Spirit! Dishonesty does not pay! Clean your house of all lies, deception, and dishonesty, no matter the cause or form. This is another step for restoring open heavens over your home.

3. Are you speaking blessings or curses? Speak words of blessing.

Jesus said:

> *The words that I speak unto you, they are spirit, and they are life* (John 6:63b).

As discussed in the previous chapter, our words carry power and bring life or death. This puts the responsibility squarely on our shoulders to carefully consider the impact of our words. This is particularly true for the man of the house as he safeguards or reestablishes holiness in his home. If you are a man, you are responsible for the atmosphere created by the words you permit to be spoken in your home. Psalm 19:14 says:

> *Let the words of my mouth, and the meditation of*
> *my heart, be acceptable in thy sight, O Lord, my*
> *strength, and my redeemer.*

We need to remember that our mouths continually release blessings or curses into our environment. Curses are things that we don't want to come to pass, yet we speak them anyway. I used to equate the biblical concepts of prophecy and blessing. Now I know that there is a big difference between prophecy and blessing. Both are of God, but not everyone functions in the gift of prophecy. However, everyone has the ability to bless.

Even our prayers fall under this principle of blessing and cursing. At one point in my ministry, God admonished me that I was praying curses over my church because I was constantly complaining and whining that my vision for the church wasn't coming to pass. My words were accomplishing the opposite of what I yearned to see happen. Similarly, I often listed my lack during my prayer time instead of thanking God for His goodness, power, and mercy to accomplish things that I could not.

One day, Holy Spirit showed me my error. I began to pray the solution instead of the problem from that time on. I began to speak into existence those things that were not. Sure enough, I began to see those things come to pass in God's timing. It took some time to learn to speak blessings instead of curses, but Holy Spirit, the Teacher, taught me much from God's Word.

Family Blessings

The more I studied and read, the more I realized that almost everyone in the Old Testament was in the blessing business. In fact, a father's blessing during that time was so important that it was considered the most valuable part of a son's inheritance. This was particularly true for the eldest son, who was set to inherit most of his father's property. Esau was quite distraught when he discovered that Jacob deceived their father and received the blessing. *"Hast thou but one blessing, my father? bless me, even me also, O my father"*[4] were his pitiful words as he wept inconsolably.

When Jacob neared the end of his life, He blessed his sons with fatherly blessings, which followed them the rest of their lives. He spoke powerful blessings over each son and called into being those things not yet visible.

Another blessing is evident in the love story of Isaac and Rebekah, told in Genesis 24. As Rebekah was about to leave with Abraham's servant and become Isaac's wife, Laban and Bethuel gathered the entire family around Rebekah and declared as God ordained:

> *Thou art our sister, be thou the mother of thousands of millions, and let thy seed possess the gate of those which hate them* (Genesis 24:60).

How different might our daughters' lives be if we blessed them in this way as they enter a marriage covenant? How many presidents, prime ministers, generals, and others of renown would be born into our families?

Priestly Blessings

The New Testament also clarifies that God wants His people to practice a lifestyle of blessing.

> Bless them which persecute you: bless, and curse not (Romans 12:14).

This is particularly evident when Jesus sent out His disciples and commanded them to bless those homes where they were received warmly and treated graciously.

> And into whatsoever house ye enter, first say, Peace be to this house. And if the son of peace be there, your peace shall rest upon it: if not, it shall turn to you again (Luke 10:5-6).

He then said that if a city received them well, miracles and gifts of healing would manifest. But if the inhabitants rejected the Lord's servants, they were authorized to pronounce a curse on that city!

A priestly blessing is one of the most wonderful gifts a man or woman of God can give. This blessing is spoken with an unction (or anointing) over people declaring the desires we have for them. A blessing possesses the creative power of God. Powerful examples of priestly blessings also begin nearly every Epistle in the New Testament.

Speaking Blessings or Curses in Our Homes

The Bible clearly states that blessing and cursing should never come from the same mouth. Whether in blessing or cursing, the words we utter will return to us.

> *Out of the same mouth proceedeth blessing and cursing. My brethren, these things ought not so to be. Doth a fountain send forth at the same place sweet water and bitter? Can the fig tree, my brethren, bear olive berries? either a vine, figs? so can no fountain both yield salt water and fresh* (James 3:10-12).
>
> *Not rendering evil for evil, or railing for railing: but contrariwise blessing; knowing that ye are thereunto called, that ye should inherit a blessing* (1 Peter 3:9).

We often do not realize the good or damage we create with our words. If we want to be blessed, we must bless. Let me show you what I mean, using the relationship between a parent and a child.

A Father's Curse

"Come here, boy. You make me sick. You're such a deadbeat that you're never going to amount to anything. I guess you're going to get your little girlfriend pregnant, and then I'll have to take care of both of you for the rest of your lives. I can already tell that I will have to pay your bills and support your illegitimate child. You're sickening. You're not working, and you never go out and look for a job. You are the laziest person I've ever known. Other children get up and do something with their lives, and their parents are really proud of them. But you—you just make me ashamed."

A Mother's Curse

"Come here, girl. Where were you last night? Don't lie to me because I know that you were out there having sex with that guy. I know that you have already lost your virginity. Well, if you think you're going to have an illegitimate child and bring it into this house, you've got a surprise coming. Don't even bother to go places with me when that happens. I will not give those people the satisfaction of pointing at you and telling me, 'I told you so,' even though I have always said that you'd end up being a tramp."

Parents who continually speak curses over their children can only blame themselves when their predictions become self-fulfilled prophecies. What kind of a man will a 16-year-old boy become if his father constantly curses him because he believes the boy is lazy? What kind of a woman will a teenage daughter become if her mother continually tells her that she is a tramp? Their lives would be different if their parents would bless them and not curse them. How special those times would be if the parents would put their hands on their children, thank the Lord for them, and bless them in His name.

A Father's Blessing

"Come here, son. I want you to know I love you. I can sense you are going through a tough time right now. When I was your age, I had to find myself, and it wasn't easy. I still remember those rough days I went through. I want you to know that your mother and I still remember that special day when we took you to the man of God and put you in his arms. Son, that was the day we dedicated you to the Lord. I remember well the minister's prayer over you, and I have full faith in God's ability to bring that prayer to pass! He is the author and finisher of our faith. I can hardly wait for you to have a family so I can bounce your children on my knees. Those are going to be great days! But in the meantime, son, as you go through these tough days, remember that your mother and I are standing behind you with everything we've got. Don't hurry into manhood. Let God take you there in His own time. If you ever need to talk to me, you just come to me. You are my son, and I want the best for you. I'd like to take time right now to ask our Lord to continue blessing you."

A Mother's Blessing

"Come here, my daughter, and let me talk with you. I know it is hard to believe, but I remember how I felt when I was young. I was in a hurry to grow up and marry some handsome young man, and I just couldn't wait to have a baby of my own. Do you know what I discovered? I found out that young girls are supposed to dream of those things because that is the way God made us. After falling in love with your father and getting married, we both dreamed of a child. What a blessing your birth was for us! I then realized that God wanted me to be happy, and so did my parents. Honey, it's okay to dream about romance and your future husband, and it would be even better if you would start praying for him right now. Don't wait until you think you've found your young man. Pray for him now, even before you meet him. At the right time, God will bring you together. Why don't we pray for that right now? I love you, honey. By the way, you're going to make a great wife and mother."

God longs to see godly fathers and mothers bless their children and each other. Begin today to weigh your words carefully before you release the power they carry. This is one thing you can do to clean up a sterile house. If you've been speaking curses—either purposefully or unintentionally—begin this moment to speak blessings! Ask God to forgive you as you break all the curses you've spoken. Repent and begin a life of speaking blessings.

4. Is there anything that holds power over you? Free your home of the power of sin.

There is a difference between the *penalty of sin* and the *power of sin*. Most Christians worry about the penalty of sin, but they need to be more concerned about the power of sin. By concerning themselves primarily with the penalty of sin, they focus more on the outcome of their lives than on the influences in their lives. They work hard to avoid hell but give little thought to the attitudes, thoughts, and behaviors that sin implants in their lives.

If this is true for you, you may try many tactics not to get caught—whether it is cheating on your income tax, cheating your boss, or cheating on your spouse—while using little or no effort to change the cheating patterns in your life. You have forgotten you cannot hide your cheating from God. He has caught you whether the government, your boss, or your spouse catches you. A reckoning with yourself comes when you ask, "Why am

I hiding, and what power is causing me to sneak around, disguise my actions, lie about my whereabouts, and cheat?" The answer is—the power of sin. Sin is holding you captive!

The penalty of your sin has been dealt with if you have received Jesus Christ as your Savior. His blood covers everything you confess and repent of. Now, ask yourself this question and answer honestly: "Does a particular sin I confessed still exert power over my life?" In other words, are you still lying? Do you still feel driven to exaggerate the truth to justify your behavior? Are you still bitter over the wrong you suffered long ago?

"Well, Brother Kilpatrick," you may say, "I asked God to forgive me because I want to go to Heaven. My sin is now under the blood." This may be true, but you still haven't answered the question: Does sin still have power over you?

Most alcoholics hate what they do, and many are quick to repent of the sins committed while they are drunk. They sincerely ask God to forgive them and save their souls. This is all very good, but forgiveness does not break the power of alcoholism. Until the power of alcoholism is broken, they will regularly need to deal with the penalty of their sin. Indeed, if they persist in their alcoholic patterns, they may well end up being worse off than before they asked God to forgive them.

I want you to understand this: God has the power not only to forgive any sins you have committed but also to break every damnable thing that has a death grip on your life. Nothing is too hard for Him! If you are an alcoholic, drug addict, child abuser, pornography addict, liar, habitual gambler—a slave to whatever sin has taken over your life—God's Spirit can permanently break the chains of that sin so that it no longer has power over you. No matter what has you bound, whether an eating disorder, anger, or lust, God can free you for life! Sin shall not have dominion over you.

> *Let not sin therefore reign in your mortal body, that ye should obey it in the lusts thereof. ...For sin shall not have dominion over you: for ye are not under the law, but under grace* (Romans 6:12,14).

Perhaps you are in bondage to the devil himself. You still have the power of choice. You can choose today to confess all your weaknesses, fears, and inabilities to Jesus Christ. You can forsake the sin that has become an unbearable weight. Jesus will meet you as surrender.

You are a product of your choices. Make the right choices, and you will be free, no matter what Satan's tactics are now or in the future. You can rid your heart and your home of the power of sin. It is a crucial step in clearing and keeping clear the heavens over your home. Jesus will unleash the power of Heaven to set you free! Be careful to guard all that He cleanses.

5. Is your home under a curse? Destroy those things that act as beacons to draw demons to your home.

According to international law, any foreign embassy's land, buildings, and property are part of that nation, whether in the United States or abroad. That is why oppressed people under authoritarian regimes, or caught between warring factions, often flee to U.S. embassies and seek asylum. If they stay at the embassy, even in a communist country, their rights and protection are the same as if they were standing on the lawn of the White House in Washington, D.C. The U.S. embassies in foreign countries are considered to be American soil.

Now picture this in reverse. When you keep the property of Satan's dark empire in your house, you have given him the legal right to establish his presence in your home! In essence, you have given him an embassy, and he can send his demons into your home because he has a legal right to operate through whatever property he owns.

With that sobering truth in mind, I encourage you to rid your house of all things that belong to Satan. Perhaps you have saved ungodly pictures, articles, or coarse jokes from social media. Maybe some of the trinkets on your tables or shelves, the images that grace your walls, or the jewelry that adorns your or your spouse's neck have demonic origins. Perhaps you own Ouija boards, pentagrams, astrological charts, tarot cards, or books and media that promote witchcraft. These things are rooted in the occult and act like lightning rods for demonic spirits!

If instruments of darkness and the occult are in your house, I guarantee they will attract demonic activity. Like draws like. The dark powers that inspire popular media, games, symbols, and divination tools call mighty demonic forces in the heavens, inviting them to enter your home. These powers gratefully accept the invitation, and soon green and red streaks run along your walls. You may not notice them, or you may not even believe these things are evil, but this does not change who and what they represent. You have given Satan entrance into your house. God sees this even if you do not—or will not. He knows precisely the items in your home that are causing pollution. Some things may be hidden. Others are set out on display. Wherever they are, these beacons draw unwelcome and unpleasant company into your home. Get rid of these demonic lightning rods if you are serious about cleansing your home and opening the heavens over yourself and your family.

6. Is Satan coming into your home through what you listen to and watch? Stop allowing ungodly and polluted material to enter your home through modern technology.

In ancient times, the devil was often carried into kingdoms and villages in the form of grand idols. These idols were carried on the shoulders of frenzied worshipers willing to sacrifice even their children. The devil loved these processions that gave him easy access to establish his kingdom. Satan does not need golden idols or grand processions to access our homes. He uses an even more effective vehicle for evil—modern media! Satan throws a saddle over the airwaves, locks his feet in the stirrups, and rides right into your home through modern technology. He lands on your floor and goes to work. In particular, children are susceptible to his invasion since millions of parents have abandoned them to the care of TVs, smartphones, and computers.

I'm not one to advocate throwing out your electronic devices—just control them! Many parents are unaware of the demonic activity available through apps and programs available at the push of a button. Many of these programs contain witchcraft, vulgarity, and obscene material.

I am continually shocked by the filthy, polluted things Christians permit to enter their homes. Even Lot was able to keep the Sodomites out of his home, but today, people allow demons full access right into their homes through media. Millions of Christian homes are filled with R-rated movies that continually contaminate their environment with repeated mantras of G—d— this and s—of a b— that.

Are you hooked on pornography? Are you or someone in your home secretly using a smartphone to access lewd videos or photographs? If you are aware of anything ungodly invading your home, it's time to clean house. There are green and red streaks on your walls. You do not need a preacher, or anyone as far as that goes, to censor what you watch or engage with online. You know in your heart when something is sinful. The Holy Spirit will let you know.

Start purging your home of the plague that has overcome you. Clean out everything that invites Satan's presence and influence in your home. Change your family's future by making the right choices now. Then, and only then, will your brass skies become clear, and your sterile house become fertile. Then, and only then, as you rigorously and honestly deal with the sin in your house, will the anointing of God fill your home and bless your family so that you will be continually bathed by His loving presence. The heavens are open to those who carefully assess the condition of their homes and take the necessary steps to establish holiness and freedom.

Endnotes

1. See John 5:19.
2. See Matthew 10:21; Romans 1:30.
3. See Exodus 20:8-11.
4. Genesis 27:38.

CHAPTER 8

REAPING UNDER AN OPEN HEAVEN

Before the turn of the century in New York City harbor, all shipping had to pass through a notorious navigation channel called Hell Gate. This passage, which ran between the Bronx and Long Island, was perilous because of treacherous currents and a cluster of rocks called Flood Rock that jutted upright in the middle of the shipping lane. Even though incoming ship captains approached Hell Gate cautiously, hundreds of ships were destroyed, and many lives were lost over the years. It is said that the passage got its name from the old sailors' saying, "Many a godless man has entered hell through that awful gate."

Exasperated city fathers finally brought in engineers to study the problem. In 1885, they placed explosive charges around Flood Rock to blast the obstruction out of the channel. Ignition wires were strung through town to the mayor's office at city hall, where they connected them to a switch. The extra effort was made because the event had aroused the population's interest and attracted press attention worldwide.

On October 10th, the mayor and his small daughter met with two witnesses and a group of newspaper reporters and photographers in his office. After announcing to the press that the switch in his office would detonate the explosive charges that would blast a wider channel through Hell Gate, he suddenly acted on a whim and turned to his little daughter. "Honey, why don't you engage the switch and set off the blast?" This little girl was thrilled to be with her daddy, but she knew nothing about ships or tides. She was utterly ignorant of the technical arrangements, and she barely understood what all the fuss was about. But when her father said, "Do it, honey," she obeyed and closed the electrical switch as the reporters watched.

The people who observed her didn't see any fireworks in the mayor's office that day. They were standing in a building at the heart of the city, far from Hell Gate channel in New York harbor. None of the people in that room saw or heard the explosive eruptions that rocked the harbor immediately after the little girl closed the switch. They simply trusted that all would happen as it had been planned, a trust that was vindicated when the phone rang a few minutes later and an exultant voice on the other end of the line said just five words: "Hell Gate is no more!" To this day, if you drive near New York City harbor, you will see road signs still bearing the name "Hell Gate," but its geographic namesake was destroyed more than a century ago.

A little girl's act of obedience with dainty fingers blasted away the treacherous rocky outcropping that had once taken many lives and blocked the shipping channel into the most significant harbor in the United States. It took only a simple act of childlike obedience to unleash the earth-shattering power that destroyed Hell Gate. Today, God wants to destroy the spiritual gates of hell[1] that still exert significant influence on the affairs of men. If we obey Him with the faith of a child, He will release His unlimited power against every ungodly force that is hardening the skies over our heads and plaguing our homes. This is the miracle and mystery of the Cross—even harlots, thieves, backsliders, and little children can release heaven's incredible power by repenting, obeying, and submitting to God. It's not *our strength* that moves the stones of bondage entombing our lives; it is the power of Christ released through our humble obedience.

The Gates of Hell Shall Not Prevail

Many Christians have never really grasped what Jesus was saying when He said, *"upon this rock I will build My church; and the gates of hell shall not prevail against it."*[2] Let's take an in-depth look at "gates" in Scripture. Gates in ancient times were focal points of power.

- Business was conducted at the city gates. Boaz took off his shoe and gave it to the city officials at the gate, officially indicating that he was redeeming Ruth's possessions.[3]

- Military strategy was planned at the gates. It was said that a city would be open and vulnerable if the gates could be taken.[4]

- Judgments and punishment were delivered at the gates.[5]

- The husband of a virtuous woman was known in the gates.[6]

- Abraham's nephew, Lot, sat at the gates of Sodom as an elder.[7]

- The strength of its gates determined the safety of a city. If the enemy stormed the gates and succeeded, his horses, chariots, and machinery of war could then enter.[8]

- When the gates came down, the city was conquered.[9]

Right now, in the spirit realm, there are evil magistrates, rulers, and elders "sitting at gates" all over the world plotting, scheming, strategizing, and planning to prevent our churches and our homes from achieving any kind of breakthrough in the heavens. They even craft plans to contaminate businesses and social structures to further their twisted agenda of devilish destruction. Right in the face of this darkness, Jesus, the Light of the world, said that the "gates of hell" will *not* prevail against His Church. They will not prevent, overpower, block, overwhelm, outlast, or win against His Church.

What Is a Gate?

A gate is "an opening in a wall or fence; a city or castle entrance often with defensive structures (as towers); a means of entrance or exit; an area for departure or arrival, a door, valve, or other mechanisms for controlling passage; a device that outputs a signal when specified input conditions are met."[10]

Where Are Hell's Gates?

Now that we have defined what a "gate" is, we need to understand what Jesus meant by "gates of hell." The Scriptures describe hell in at least three contexts:

1. Hell is a literal place or region in the underworld where God will ultimately incarcerate Satan, the fallen angels who followed Satan into rebellion, and the souls of humans who chose to reject God's Son as their Savior and Lord.

2. Hell can describe a condition. James 3:6 says:

   And the tongue is a fire, a world of iniquity: so is the tongue among our members, that it defileth the whole body, and setteth on fire the course of nature; and it is set on fire of hell.

   This picture of a tongue ignited by the fire of hell also gives us a vivid picture of hell itself.

3. "Hell's gate" refers to Satan's earthly seat of power as manifested in the heavens of brass he creates over the heads of men who consistently disobey God and willfully live in sin. (This does not refer to the gaseous atmosphere surrounding this planet, nor the high heavens where God Almighty abides on His throne. Satan was cast down from the high heavens.)

Satan is not in hell yet. The Bible says he is the *"prince of this world"*[11] and the *"prince of the power of the air, the spirit that now worketh in the children of disobedience."*[12] He commands the *"rulers of the darkness of this world,"*[13] and he is still on the loose. John, the apostle, told the Church that *"the whole world lieth in* [under the power of] *wickedness."*[14]

So, when Jesus talks about the gates of hell, He's not referring to a set of red-hot, smoking, steel-barred gates located in the fire and brimstone dungeons of Hades. That place does indeed exist, and it is waiting for the arrival of the chained serpent and his fallen angels, but it has no power over the Church. Only its eternally damned inhabitants will suffer it. Jesus was not talking about gates in the underworld. He was speaking of devilish gates in the heavens over our heads, where Satan, the adversary, actively works to obstruct the dealings of men with God.

Powers and Principalities in Heavenly Places

The Book of Daniel reveals that Satan's "angels" actively work to hinder, steal, or delay God's answers to the prayers of men. While the devil is powerless to hinder, steal from, or delay God, he does have the ability to hinder our prayers *when we allow him* to do it. Paul, the apostle, laid out the structure of Satan's forces in his Epistle to the Ephesians. One of the first things you should notice is that "powers and principalities" are always used together when referring to Satan's dark princedom.

> *For we wrestle not against flesh and blood, but against principalities, against powers, against the rulers of the darkness of this world, against spiritual wickedness in high places* (Ephesians 6:12).

190

To the intent that now unto the principalities and powers in heavenly places might be known by the church the manifold wisdom of God (Ephesians 3:10).

For I am persuaded, that neither death, nor life, nor angels, nor principalities, nor powers...shall be able to separate us from the love of God, which is in Christ Jesus our Lord (Romans 8:38-39).

And having spoiled principalities and powers, he made a shew of them openly, triumphing over them in it (Colossians 2:15).

If you study the word *principalities,* you will discover that it comes from the Greek word *arche,* which means "first, beginning, chief, and master."[15] Our modem word *architect* comes from that same Greek root, with the Greek word for *builder* being added. Satan's evil principalities are intelligent architects, builders, and engineers of evil. They study us—our homes, churches, and localities—just like an engineer studies topography or structure. Then they craft a scheme or plan, just like an architect designs blueprints for a building or a general lays out battle plans for his troops. Once the plan has been determined, the principalities bring in the "powers," the devilish muscle, to do the dirty work.

When Brownsville Assembly of God was being constructed in Pensacola, the architects used to come around from time to time with stacks of plans, blueprints, and schematics. They had envisioned and drawn the plans for the building to guide the masons, carpenters, plumbers, electricians, and painters who did the work. Once the ground was broken, I seldom saw the architects or engineers. They were tucked away downtown somewhere. What I did witness every day were the workers. I'd hear the roar of trucks going and coming, the thud of hammers, the hum of saws, and the other noises made by busy laborers carrying out the bidding of the architects who were far removed from the actual work.

The *gates of hell* are where Satan's architects and intelligent principalities devise their schemes, plans, and strategies to stop Christians. Their chief goal is to isolate our churches and homes by shutting the heavens over our heads, a task they accomplish by seducing, tricking, or persuading us to fall into various sins and acts of disobedience. Wise principalities know the right moves needed to distract, discourage, and dishearten us. After they lay the plan, they call on demonic powers to carry out their schemes. Once the battle begins, we better have our minds made up to persevere and must be wearing the whole armor of God because it will be a royal battle! But remember Jesus' promise that the gates of hell *will not prevail*—although they will most certainly assail us!

It is essential to realize you are dealing with *intelligent* schemers and mighty spiritual powers. The kingdom of darkness will pull out all the stops to silence the men or women of God who have an open heaven over their heads. They will do anything to stop the believer who is trying to punch holes in his skies of brass; therefore, Satan has us under surveillance.

Satan doesn't attack everyone the same way or with the same intensity. In fact, *the devil is not concerned with most Christians.*

They are not a threat because their lives are up and down, in and out, hot and cold. Their lukewarm walk has pretty much neutralized their effectiveness in the Kingdom of God, so Satan's minions do not even blink when they get out of bed in the morning! Some people whine and complain to anyone who will listen, "The devil's been on my back all week." No, he hasn't! They are not even worthy of a worn-out demon! They are high-maintenance, low-impact Christians who always need pampering, coddling, reassurance, and recognition. Satan's not worried about them at all.

There was one person who attracted the personal attention of the devil. After a 40-day fast in the wilderness, this man was confronted by Satan himself. Jesus posed such a threat that the devil didn't dare send just any imp or low-ranking power, or even a principality or a bull demon. Satan himself came to find out who had such a clear and yielding heaven over His head. He discovered he was dealing with Jesus Christ, the only begotten Son of God, who came in the flesh. When, without success, he dangled before the last Adam every temptation he had used to bring down the first Adam, the prince of hell knew he was in big trouble. The last Adam passed every test with flying colors.

The kingdom of darkness was in such desperate straits that Satan even picked up Jesus and took Him to the pinnacle of the Temple. Then the prince of the power of the air offered the Prince of Peace all the kingdoms of the world if He would just worship him. This earned him a stinging rebuke from God's Word, which reminded him who was his Maker and Judge.

Jesus moved in absolute obedience, and the heavens were pried wide open over His head. Hell was in a panic over Jesus.

Just as the gates of hell could not prevent, overpower, block, overwhelm, or prevail over Christ in the wilderness or on the Cross, neither will they prevail over His blood-washed Church. *But the key is obedience.* An obedient walk before God keeps the heavens open, and Satan can do nothing to close them. Bless the Lord; it's time that snake gets in a panic over this last-day Church!

I want all of hell to tremble as the heavens break open over this nation and worldwide. I want hell's denizens to panic as God's anointing sizzles, His glory falls, revival fire races, miraculous healings manifest, and mighty deliverances explode one after another!

I know the Scriptures say that evil will get worse and worse, and I believe that the events of the end times are still on schedule, but God said that *where sin abounds, His grace abounded much more.*[16] We've tried everything this world and Satan had to offer, but they've only left us empty.

I believe that some of the greatest exploits in the Kingdom are right before us. Take courage, saints! God's Word promises us even more than the power to prevail:

> *Thus saith the Lord to his anointed, to Cyrus, whose right hand I have holden, to subdue nations before him; and I will loose the loins of kings, to open before him the two leaved gates; and the gates shall not be shut; I will go before thee, and make the crooked places straight: I will break in pieces the*

gates of brass, and cut in sunder the bars of iron: and I will give thee the treasures of darkness, and hidden riches of secret places, that thou mayest know that I, the Lord, which call thee by thy name, am the God of Israel (Isaiah 45:1-3).

God said some very important things to Cyrus, the king of Persia. He said that He would cause a king (King Belshazzar of Babylon) to open the two-leaved gates, and those gates would not be shut. He said that He would break up the gates of brass and cut apart the bars of iron. Then God said He would give Cyrus the treasures of darkness and the hidden riches of secret places. What a powerful Scripture!

I realize that this Scripture passage was fulfilled when the armies of King Cyrus invaded Babylon and captured it in one night. But this event from Daniel's day also contains a great spiritual truth. God used the Babylonian empire to punish Israel for its apostasy and idolatry. Their national sin had opened them up to spiritual and physical captivity. All the riches of Jerusalem were plundered and carried away to the hidden treasure houses of Babylon. Her finest young men and women were stolen to serve ungodly kings in a distant land. Even her temple of worship and sacrifice was destroyed, and the national identity of the Jews was eliminated. Still, even after decades of captivity, there was a longing in the hearts of God's people for a homeland and a wonderful reunion with their God.

God raised Cyrus up to conquer the mighty Babylonian empire in answer to their prayers. Once this had happened, Cyrus released the Jews to return to their homeland, precisely as God prophesied through Isaiah. God then moved on the Persian king of Nehemiah's day to allow the Jews to rebuild Jerusalem and restore her walls. Without the Jews raising even one weapon of war, God sovereignly moved to deliver His captive nation by raising up one empire to destroy another. The Jews' part in this affair was to obey.

Where Are My Goods, Devil?

Have you ever asked yourself, "Am I *missing* something? Where are the things Satan has stolen from me?" These stolen things are *still in existence* somewhere, even though you can't see them. When Satan steals our blessings, he doesn't destroy them because he doesn't have the power or authority to do so. He locks away these "treasures of darkness and hidden riches of secret places." These stolen and hidden goods are *our treasures.*

What then are these treasures and riches? We know from God's Word that *"every good gift and every perfect gift is from above, and cometh down from the Father of lights, with whom is no variableness, neither shadow of turning."*[17] How are the treasures of darkness different from the gifts and treasures of God, who is light?

They are "treasures of darkness" because the enemy has tucked them away in the secret treasure chests of his dark realm. Satan stole them by keeping our blessings from us, but God wants them back. Therefore, He promises to *"break in pieces the gates of brass and cut in sunder the bars of iron."* God is plundering Satan's treasure chests to restore what was seized by theft and deception.

Satan locked up the treasures of Daniel and Israel when he made the heavens brass above their heads, but Daniel's 21 days of persistent prayer brought heavenly action. An angel appeared to Daniel and said:

> *Fear not, Daniel: for from the first day that thou didst set thine heart to understand, and to chasten thyself before thy God, thy words were heard...* (Daniel 10:12).

God heard Daniel immediately, but Daniel still had to persevere in prayer until the angel appeared and said:

> *...I am come for thy words* (Daniel 10:12).

Beginning in Daniel 10:12, the Scriptures show how the angel pulled aside the veil that separates the realm of flesh from that of eternal spirit. He gave Daniel keen insight into the battles of heavenly princes and our prayers' crucial role in their outcomes.

Four Results of Daniel's Prayers

1. Prayer brought heavenly action.

Every child of God should be excited when he sees that Daniel's prayers were heard and acted upon the *first day* he fell to his knees and prayed. *Every single prayer offered in obedience and purity is heard and answered by God!*[18] However, these answers are not always immediately visible. God ordained some answers to be fulfilled by fervent unyielding prayer, just as the one delivered to Daniel.

2. Prayer unlocked information.

Daniel learned vital information in four areas—the future of the Jewish people, the power of his prayer and the instant response God gave it, the nature of spiritual warfare in the heavenlies, and God's opinion of him as an individual.[19]

The angel gave Daniel one of the Bible's most far-reaching and detailed prophecies concerning future world events. This prophecy covers a large segment of world history.

3. Prayer unlocked angelic help.

The warrior-prince from heaven told Daniel, *"I am come for thy words."*[20] It was Daniel's prayer that provoked the divine dispatch of angelic force and support for Daniel and his nation. His continuing prayer unleashed the formidable power of Michael, the archangel who assisted in bringing to Daniel God's answer to his prayer. Daniel's prayer unleashed the hounds of heaven on the demonic prince of Persia.

Please note that these heavenly beings were not like the tame variety of angels we usually imagine. The angel told Daniel:

> *Now will I return to fight with the prince of Persia*
> (Daniel 10:20a).

That Hebrew word, *lacham*, literally means "to feed on; to consume (figuratively), to devour, overcome, prevail."[21] Daniel was in the presence of a very warlike angel who fought to win!

4. Prayer unlocked supernatural strength.

At the time of the angel's appearance, Daniel was already weakened from 21 days of a partial fast and constant intercessory prayer over his heartbreaking burden. The appearance and voice of the angel caused him to faint, making him unable to receive the angelic message. Part of the angel's assignment was to strengthen the man of God, just as angels ministered to Jesus after His 40-day fast and confrontation with the devil. The angel touched Daniel's body three times as he imparted new strength to him.[22]

Daniel moved kings, nations, and demonic principalities from his knees. We can only imagine what he might have done had he lived on this side of the Cross! Demonic strategy continues at hell's gates, but Jesus declared those gates powerless against His Church. This was guaranteed by Christ's birth, death, and resurrection and His gift of the Holy Spirit to the Church.

Nevertheless, you and I have a part to play in God's plan. Let's try to better understand our role by looking at two powerful Scriptures concerning gates:

> *That in blessing I will bless thee, and in multiplying I will multiply thy seed as the stars of the heaven, and as the sand which is upon the sea shore; and thy seed shall possess the gate of his enemies* (Genesis 22:17).

> *In that day shall the Lord of hosts be for a crown of glory, and for a diadem of beauty, unto the residue of his people, and for a spirit of judgment to him that sitteth in judgment, and for strength to them that turn the battle to the gate* (Isaiah 28:5-6).

God is interested in action based on obedience. If we *turn the battle to hell's gate,* He will supply the strength for the battle! The devil has been busy making the heavens brass by enticing us to live in sin and disobedience. He then stole our most precious treasures and locked them away. He has been incredibly slick in his campaign against the Church. He has orchestrated and schemed planned attacks while the Church, distracted by irrelevant things, has squabbled, entertained, complained, and slept its way into needless failure.

The Tide Is Turning

So many souls came to the altars at the Brownsville Revival and were born again by the Spirit of God that we had to quit counting. When the revival was in full swing, God was moving in such powerful and spontaneous ways that it was impossible to keep up with a nightly count. During the revival, a safe, conservative estimate would be that over 4.5 million people came through the doors of Brownsville Assembly of God, and hundreds of thousands were born again. This was not a man-made revival. It was initiated by God alone. He moved upon hearts and imparted a tremendous spirit of repentance and holiness.

I sat on the platform night after night and saw people, including the "chiefest of sinners," stream forward to repent and get right with God. I heard people share their stories of past woes, misery, and anguish, and I heard people give glory to God about experiencing peace, joy, and true rest after coming to Jesus. I have personally seen the impact that Holy Ghost revival has on a church, city, and the nations of the earth. Despite every effort of Satan, when God sends revival, it will come with power and glory, and the gates of hell will not prevail!

Because of the mighty move of God experienced at Brownsville, we became determined to retrieve the treasures of darkness that Satan has locked away. We continue to pursue the return of the riches he stashed in secret places—our rest, peace, joy, blessings, happy homes, children, ministries, anointing, and our health and well-being.

Satan knows his time is limited. Every day that goes by, he has fewer and fewer days, which means he will become more and more active. Seemingly, the only deterrent to the flood tide of sin and rebellion is revival and possibly a great awakening. Church as usual has never gotten and will not get the job done. It will take a spontaneous move of the Holy Spirit to stop the flood tide Satan has planned.

The New Testament reveals that Jesus was *ruthless* with the devil and his hierarchy. The Lord stayed on the Cross and tenaciously held out until He knocked the crown from Satan's head. He persevered until He had personally invaded the underworld, preached to the captives, and snatched the keys of death and hell from Lucifer's trembling grip.

Jesus took the arrows of death and broke them in half. He forever removed the sting of death, and He did it through obedience. Jesus Christ spoiled the devil's powers and principalities, making "a show of them openly."[23] He was merciless. If you think He caused a commotion when He spilled the take of the money changers in the temple courts, imagine what He did when He openly made a show of Satan. It will be interesting to see all the losses hell will experience in the coming days!

Some people in the Church have slow danced with the devil, but a generation is arising that will have nothing to do with compromise. They are a new breed of believers and have fire in their eyes and swords in their hands.

Centuries ago, Jesus told Peter and the disciples:

> And I will give unto thee the keys of the kingdom of heaven (Matthew 16:19a).

This new generation will storm hell's gates and do more than binding and loosing. They will not settle for the halfway measures like King Joash:

> And Elisha said unto [King Joash], Take bow and arrows. And he took unto him bow and arrows. And he said to the king of Israel, Put thine hand upon the bow. And he put his hand upon it: and Elisha put his hands upon the king's hands. And he said, Open the window eastward. And he opened it. Then Elisha said, Shoot. And he shot. And he said, The arrow of the Lord's deliverance, and the arrow of deliverance from Syria: for thou shalt smite the Syrians in Aphek, till thou have consumed them. And he said, Take the arrows. And he took them. And he said unto the king of Israel, Smite upon the ground. And he smote thrice, and stayed. And the man of God was wroth with him, and said, Thou shouldest have smitten five or six times; then

hadst thou smitten Syria till thou hadst consumed
it: whereas now thou shalt smite Syria but thrice
(2 Kings 13:15-19).

Elisha instructed the window to be opened eastward toward Syria, the direction from which the attack would come. Then the prophet put his hands on Joash's hands, signifying that the source of prophetic authority, the Holy Spirit, was empowering Joash to shoot the arrow toward Syria. After telling Joash that God wanted him to destroy the Syrian army, Elisha told the king to strike the ground with the arrows. When Joash only struck the ground three times, Elisha was angry over the king's timidity in war. In essence, he said, "You should have struck the ground five or six times. Then you would have battled with Syria until you had destroyed it. Now, you will defeat Syria only three times. Watch out!"

In my mind's eye, I see a generation, unlike King Joash, that will unashamedly point a handful of God's arrows directly toward the heavens of brass and treasures of darkness. I can hear the Holy Spirit say, "Shoot! Now, strike the ground!" This generation will not be bashful or intimidated. They will move headlong into the enemy's camp and take back *all* the devil has stolen. They will be ruthless and settle for nothing less than complete and absolute victory over the enemy!

I believe this powerful new band of mighty warriors will not allow religion to stifle them. As the Holy Ghost helps and works with them, they will boldly dare to do last-day exploits. I long to see the Church arise from her slumber and violently turn back the battle toward the gates of hell. We have the unlimited

203

power of Heaven behind us. It is written in the Book and sealed in Jesus' blood! The tide of God's glory will rise!

May we soon hear the words ring out, *"The gates of hell are no more!"*

Endnotes

1. The author acknowledges his indebtedness to Dick Bernal's discussion of hell's gates in *Storming Hell's Brazen Gates* (San Jose, CA: Jubilee Christian Center, 1988).

2. Matthew 16:18.

3. See Ruth 4:1-11.

4. See Obadiah 1:11.

5. See Deuteronomy 17:5.

6. Proverbs 31:23.

7. See Genesis 19:1.

8. See 2 Chronicles 14:7.

9. See Nehemiah 1:3.

10. *Merriam Webster's Collegiate Dictionary*, 482.

11. John 16:11.

12. Ephesians 2:2.

13. Ephesians 6:12.

14. 1 John 5:19.

15. Strong's, *arche* (Gr., #746).

16. See Romans 5:20.

17. James 1:17.

18. See John 15:16; 16:23-24.

19. See Daniel 10:10-12; 12:13.

20. Daniel 10:12b.

21. Strong's, *fight* (Heb., #3898).

22. See Daniel 10:10,16,18.

23. Colossians 2:15.

ABOUT JOHN KILPATRICK

John Kilpatrick was blessed to experience the glory of God as the Holy Spirit entrusted him with the pastoral oversight of the historic Brownsville Revival in Pensacola, Florida, and the Bay Revival in Mobile, Alabama. He currently serves as the founder and executive pastor of Church of His Presence in Daphne, Alabama. He also travels across the nation, spreading the fires of revival and impacting churches worldwide through media ministry. With over 50 years of pastoral ministry, 22 of which included his ministry at Brownsville Assembly of God in Pensacola, he and his wife, Brenda, are fulfilling their apostolic call by helping to establish churches and mentoring ministers.